Every Woman Has '5' Men . . . To Choose From

LEEDS

PUBLISHING HOUSE

ISBN 979-8-89766-852-6

Table of Contents

Introduction

Love and relationships have always been complex, but choosing the right partner has unique challenges for women. In today's world, the societal expectations placed on women, their romantic ideals, and their desires in what they seek from a mate often conflict with them, Leading many women into cycles of heartbreaks, confusion, and disappointment. But what if I told you that **"Every Woman Has Five Men to Choose From?"** Thus, understanding these 'five' options can make the difference between settling for less or securing a fulfilling, lasting relationship.

We all know that for every woman, there is 'one' man who can foot the bill. But where and how to find him . . . is the issue. So, let's dig a little deeper.

One of the main challenges that women face in dating is essentially understanding how men genuinely think beyond the most typical presumption that men only desire physical intimacy or sex from women. To successfully navigate relationships, women must first accept and learn how men communicate, relate, and process their emotions. These minuscule or enormous differences often lead to misunderstandings and frustrations between men and women.

For example, a man's innate desire for sex is primarily driven by biological and hormonal factors. This is important to understand because when a man initially expresses interest in a woman, it is often to explore only the possibility of physical intimacy rather than emotional intimacy or the presumptive or immediate commitment to a relationship.

I have heard some women say, "All he wants from me is sex," and in many cases, this may be true—because most men choose to prioritize sex. A man's initial attraction to a woman doesn't indicate his wanting to build a forever future together. His initial attraction to her is merely premised on the idea of hope. He hopes that she might allow physical intimacy to occur and that she might find him reciprocally attractive, and only after that does he even begin to consider the prospective concept of a deeper connection.

As previously mentioned, the baseless misconception that when a man approaches a woman, he is automatically interested in a committed relationship, unfortunately, isn't true. In those first few moments, a man will engage with a woman out of curiosity. His inherent attraction to her is to analyze whether she aligns with what 'he wants.'

Let's be honest—if a man realizes a woman isn't his type or doesn't see a future with her, do you think he'll come right out and tell her that? Most likely not. Why? Because he doesn't want to eliminate the possibility of becoming physically intimate with her. It sounds harsh, but that's just one of the unspoken rules regarding male and female interactions.

In truth, a man may enjoy a woman's company, find her attractive, or even appreciate aspects of her personality. However, even if he doesn't feel like she's the one, he still won't automatically walk away from his current relationship or connect with a new woman in 'a situationship.' Instead, he'll seek to buy time—while decisively keeping things open-ended to see where the relationship or 'situationship' leads, especially if there's a promise of physical intimacy impending or currently occurring between them.

Now, let's contrast that with women. Some younger women may take a similar approach. They might also want to explore their options by keeping things casual and avoiding commitment with just one man. On the other hand, for most mature women, the stakes are usually different. They've outgrown the uncertainty of the dating world and aren't looking for temporary, fruitless, or fleeting connections. These women seek real commitment, stability, and a long-term relationship— not just momentary romances or overnight flings.

A woman might very well agree to date a man she isn't immediately or necessarily attracted to while giving herself time to see if her attraction to him or her initial feelings for him change. She may do so and continue dating him while keeping her other potential suitors and prospects in mind, thus allowing her rational mind to decide if he's the right fit. The real question is not whether this behavior is right or wrong but rather about the timing and circumstances.

A woman in an uncertain and tentative relationship with 'one' man might start seeing another man under her subjective convictions that her current partner isn't showing the necessary signs of commitment she needs. This may lead her to go on dates searching for her idea of the right partner while believing she is just lightly keeping her options open. But the truth is that most men are doing the same thing she is doing. They, too, are testing the waters and exploring the field.

However, this strategy seldom works. Ultimately, it often leads to discontent and disappointment because it lacks genuine depth and sincere intentions. Women seeking to date casually while keeping their options open may think they're protecting themselves. Still, they often feel frustrated, jaded, bitter, and resentful.

Take this scenario, for example: a woman meets the perfect partner—someone who embodies everything she's always desired. Yet, because she chooses to keep her options open, she hesitates, entertains distractions, or worse... fails to recognize his value in the moment. Before she even realizes it, he's gone.

This is where relational regret and bitterness take root— when the one who got away becomes the one she can't stop thinking about.

So, as time passes and the reality of aging sets in, some women may feel the pressure to *redeem time*. This impossible attempt often leads to women issuing ultimatums before a relationship blossoms, grows, or develops. When we're younger, time feels abundant. It offers us the idea and notion of freedom that there's perpetual room for exploration. However, as we grow older, we realize and recognize that time is a precious resource—we don't have the luxury to waste it. This shift in mindset inspires us to become more intentional, especially when it comes to relationships.

Yet, here lies the challenge: The new man a woman meets has nothing to do with her past. However, if she seeks to bring up commitment and marriage too early in the "just getting to know each other" or "dating phase," it can inadvertently cause the man to pull back.

Men can sense the *weight* behind a woman's urgency when a long-term commitment or marriage is mentioned too soon. Often at times, if a man hears something like, *"I'm looking for something serious"* early on, unfortunately for the woman, he may instinctively interpret it as desperation—especially if it feels like she's rushing to secure only the status or 'idea' of being in a relationship. Even if that's not her actual intention to come off as desperate or goal-driven, typical men, being logical thinkers, often believe that someone genuinely seeking a lasting connection would allow the relationship to grow organically rather than forcing or rushing into commitment too quickly.

Similarly, a red flag for many men is the idea of rushing into commitment or some unrealistic relational permanence being presented by the woman—who, in meeting him after two weeks, is discussing marriage by the third. Yet, because most men avoid emotional confrontation, they won't necessarily walk away immediately when unduly presented with such commitment pressures early on. Instead, they might stay to buy time, keeping their options open while not ruining their chances of finally achieving physical intimacy or continuing the consistent receipt.

Upon meeting a woman, a man would likely never admit that the woman standing before him is not even his type. The first reason for this is simple. As discussed, he simply does not want to ruin and jeopardize the possibility of physical intimacy or sex. Suppose a man has low self-esteem or has been rejected often. In that case, he's even less likely to turn down an opportunity to physically connect with a woman, even if he knows deep down that she's not the one for him. However, if he is considered a high-value man—whether due to his looks, success, or social status—he is more likely to be upfront and tell her he's not interested in her. That said, even if he doesn't necessarily see a romantic future with her, he may keep her around as a 'friend,' especially if he notices that she is interested in him.

To be honest, the typical man generally doesn't feel comfortable rejecting women. However, when a man is what society considers *average*, his dating options are somewhat more limited. These men tend to operate with a *scarcity mindset*, meaning they don't always select partners based purely on their ideal looks, appearance, or body type preferences. While they may have a preference in mind, they also recognize that getting a date can be a struggle. Therefore, rather than holding out for a perfect match or his perfect someone, the man will be more likely to settle for whoever is available to him or reciprocates.

Women, on the other hand, tend to approach relationships entirely differently. Many women commit to a relationship with the belief that they can *change* or *improve* aspects of their partner over time. When things don't work out in the relationship, the woman often leaves, hoping to find a better-suited or more compatible partner.

While men are the exact opposite, so when men commit, they generally seek and intend to *make it work*—even if they stumble along the way with issues like unfaithfulness or temptation. For men, logic and reasoning often take precedence over emotions and feelings. Men consider the time, effort, and material investments they've put into the relationship, making them less likely to walk away impulsively or irrationally.

This fundamental difference in how men and women *perceive* relationships creates one of the biggest challenges in dating. While women may be quick to move on in search of something better, men, particularly those who feel their options are limited, will do and say whatever it takes to keep a woman interested—even if that means stretching the truth or avoiding full disclosure and honesty.

Average men typically experience rejection far more frequently than their more conventionally attractive or successful counterparts. This scarcity mindset is deeply ingrained from childhood, shaping how they interact with women. For many, simply having a woman's attention is a victory. Even if they know she isn't the one per se, rejecting her outright feels like throwing away a viable opportunity. Because of this, the man may pretend to be interested or attracted to her when he is not.

Additionally, men don't openly reject women because of the discomfort they experience in disappointing them. So, if a man finds a woman unattractive, he will not likely tell her outright. Unfortunately, this chivalry of sorts or social politeness ultimately contributes to a sense of entitlement in some women. When an average man lies to a woman about her looks or withholds his actual feedback about her overall appeal, it creates an irrevocable illusion in her that all men similarly view her the same way. Yet, this is not the case. Over time, this false validation can distort a woman's perception of herself, making her believe she holds a certain level of generalized desirability in the dating market.

You've probably seen cases where someone who lacks a specific talent or skill still carries themselves as if they are peculiarly exceptional—simply because no one ever gave them honest feedback, and they may very well not be. The same principle applies here.

From childhood, many men are nurtured by their mothers and other matriarchal figures. Thus, they develop both a natural and learned 'soft spot' for women. This is why women should attempt to recognize and discern when a man is genuinely uninterested in them and do the honorable thing by walking away from him. Men are unlikely to voluntarily step back and miss out on the opportunity for the physical intimacy goal, as discussed earlier, even if they know there's no real future in the relationship.

Moreover, an important caution to note is that some men, especially those perceived as high-value men, may not express their interest in a woman, either openly or overtly. Many high-value men, instead, enjoy the seductive power of a woman and prefer to be engaged and pursued in a way that feels organic. Unlike some men who struggle to obtain status or resources, high-value men already have money and power—whereby their primary craving is physical intimacy and the feeling of being wanted.

Since men naturally desire respect and physical intimacy, women who understand this dynamic and can skillfully use their power and the art of seduction will often attract these kinds of high-value men. However, it's essential to distinguish the above from calculated ulterior motives or from narcissism. It is imperative to remember that high-value men don't seek validation from all women but only from a specific kind of woman who intrigues them.

When a high-value man actively pursues a woman—for example, taking her on dates or showing genuine interest—it signals his heightened attraction to her. However, this delicate dance can often be easily ruined by hubris and ego, especially when both parties seek to engage in power plays like playing hard to get or a push-and-pull dynamic.

A high-value man won't chase a woman endlessly. Suppose he senses that a woman is playing games or not reciprocating his efforts. In that case, he won't waste further time proving himself. Instead, he'll dismiss the situation, assume he misjudged her interest, and respectfully move on. That's why understanding how to attract the right man is just one part of the equation—while keeping him is another challenge altogether.

This is where emotional healing and correctly interpreting a man's interest make all the difference and come into play. When past wounds cloud a woman's judgment, she may misread signals or unknowingly sabotage potential connections with the right suitor or partner. Without such clarity, the old saying—the one that got away—might become her reality.

In addition, women can enter relationships expecting men to think, feel, and communicate the way that they do, only to be left confused when things don't work out or often go as planned. Since men and women process emotions and express themselves differently, those who are not aware of this fact are likely to encounter repetitive issues from their tumultuous connections with the wrong men. To avoid misunderstandings, we must, therefore, acknowledge these differences. We are a coin with two sides. Humanity is exact.

The key to choosing the right partner isn't just about chemistry or attraction—it's about understanding how men operate and knowing which type of man aligns with your needs and values. A strong relationship isn't built on surface-level connections but on mutual understanding, shared goals, and emotional compatibility. When women take the time to recognize these differences and approach relationships with clarity, they can make more informed choices that lead to fulfilling and lasting connections.

Men's brains function in a structured, compartmentalized way. They separate different aspects of life, work, family, finances, and relationships—into mental "boxes" that don't necessarily overlap. When a man focuses on a particular subject, he retrieves the corresponding box, engages with it, and then puts it away without allowing it to affect the others. This vastly differs from how women process emotions and relationships, where everything is interconnected. A woman's thoughts, feelings, and experiences all influence one another, making it easier for her to see how different aspects of life are connected.

When a woman meets a potential partner, she is often overwhelmed with excitement and the hope of a happily ever after. She's head over heels, captivated by him, and eager to learn everything about him—how he thinks, what he wants, and all the little details that make him who he is. During this stage, her curiosity is insatiable, and physical intimacy is at its peak.

But then, reality sets in. She begins to notice imperfections she once overlooked. Some things he said no longer hold the truth she initially believed, and she may even uncover skeletons in his closet. Despite these revelations, she tries to convince herself that they can work through their differences. However, as her perception of him shifts, her emotional attraction gradually declines—dropping to about 50% of what it was in the beginning.

As the relationship continues, she starts to envision a future without him. Suppose they break up, and she begins dating again. In that case, she is more cautious, questioning whether her new partner carries the same traits that led to the downfall of her previous relationship. Her past relationship still influences her choices in many ways, guiding her selection process even if she isn't fully aware of it.

This happens because when an emotion attaches itself to a thought, that thought never truly fades. It holds power, capable of being relived as vividly today as when it first occurred—no matter how much time has passed. This is one of the fundamental differences between men and women. Men tend to compartmentalize past experiences logically, often separating them from deep emotions. On the other hand, women feel both the thought and the experience, keeping those memories alive throughout their lives. This is why women are likelier to remember special dates and moments with far greater emotional depth than men.

One of the biggest challenges women face in dating is misinterpreting how men think. For instance, men have what is often referred to as a "Nothing Box"—a mental space where they can think about absolutely nothing. This explains why a man can spend hours watching his favorite sports, sitting by a river while fishing, or endlessly scrolling through his phone without engaging in profound thoughts.

Imagine this man in a relationship with a woman whose mind is always active, constantly processing thoughts, emotions, and possibilities. She may struggle to understand his mental quiet, often mistaking his "nothingness" for disinterest, emotional detachment, or even a lack of ambition and purpose. This misunderstanding can lead to frustration and unnecessary tension in the relationship.

However, recognizing these fundamental differences can help women approach their partners more clearly and patiently. Understanding that men think differently—not less or without feeling. A man's ability to retreat into his "Nothing Box" is not a sign of indifference or a lack of love but rather a natural way he unwinds and processes life in his own way.

Throughout this book, *Every Woman Has '5' Men to Choose From*; we will successfully and interactively explore the '5' distinct types of men women encounter and how they each uniquely display characters and traits. Doing so will ultimately help and guide women to make better-informed choices in love and relationships. Just like women have unique qualities about themselves, men share the same variations of uniqueness. Ultimately, most heartbreaks seem to emerge from women simply choosing men who are not uniquely wired to meet their desires and passions in life. Summarily proving in a sentence, "One size doesn't, in fact, fit all."

After completing this book, you'll learn why some men seem perfect but lack long-term relationship potential and, most importantly, how to identify the genuinely right man for you. This isn't about playing games or changing who you are. Rather, it is about empowering yourself with the invaluable and life-altering knowledge that will help you stop wasting your time on men who do not share your values and instead choose a partner whose values, respect, and core traits match yours. I once heard someone say, "You cannot say the 'wrong' thing to the 'right' one ... and you cannot say the 'right' thing to the 'wrong 'person."

The goal of this book is simple: to help you explore the world of dating while equipping you with the confidence, clarity, and purpose you'll need to navigate the dating waters. By the time you finish reading, you'll confidently recognize the different types of men available to you and understand how to use this knowledge to build a fulfilling and lasting relationship.

This book is also designed to help women introspectively recognize the patterns in their romantic lives that directly stem from their childhood. Through this reflection and recognition, women will then understand the power and psychology of attraction, the importance of first healing from past emotional traumas, and the importance of making better-informed choices regarding love.

Through real-life scenarios, emotional insights, and practical strategies, we will explore how emotions, past experiences, and personal standards influence the men you attract and the relationships that you form.

By the end of this book, you will be able to identify the 5 types of men every woman encounters and develop the emotional intelligence and self-awareness needed to choose the right one.

This is not about fairy tale love but real love ... the kind that lasts. Whether you are single, dating, or reflecting on past relationships and marriages, this book will empower you to take control of your love life, avoid heartbreak, and build a connection that truly fulfills you.

Are you ready to take a deeper look at your romantic choices?

Let's begin.

Chapter 1

The Influence of Social Media on Modern Relationships

The internet, social media, and even reality television have dramatically changed how people experience and discuss relationships. Young people turn to online platforms for dating advice and insights and to share their private and very personal stories. Unlike in the past, where relationships were private matters, today's culture encourages oversharing—with little hesitation, even if it involves the most intimate, nuttiest, and grittiest breakup and reconciliation details of a person's experiences behind closed doors with their partner.

What was once considered deeply personal is now widely discussed. Social media has erased many privacy boundaries, making open conversations about love and dating a part of everyday life. In some ways, while this has allowed for greater awareness and shared experiences, it has also introduced newer challenges. The abundance of unvetted and unsubstantiated online content has blurred the lines between helpful advice and mere unfiltered opinions. Interestingly, younger generations tend to be more selective about what they reveal. In comparison, ironically, it is the older generations who seem to actively and openly engage in discussions on relationships, particularly around topics such as dating, courtships, engagements, infidelities, marriages, their sex life, breakups, divorces, and finding the right partner.

Sadly, one of the most painful aspects of a failed relationship is the impact on others, especially children. When two adults in a relationship decide to part ways, their children often become the ones who suffer the most as casualties of a proverbial and familial war. They didn't choose to be born into a broken household. Yet, they are left to deal with the emotional consequences and internal scars much deeper than the eye can see.

Beyond the immediate heartbreak, society often labels children statistically from broken homes, adding another layer of difficulty. As these children grow into adults, the instability they witnessed in their families shapes their views on love and relationships later in life. Sometimes, this makes it harder for them to trust or commit.

Now imagine parents who impulsively take their struggles to vent on social media, sharing their pain, frustrations, and drama with the world after a breakup. While they may need an outlet, instead of seeking help from a professional, they carelessly broadcast their private matters online. This affects their children and raises doubts about future dating prospects. Of course, we all know that bad news and sometimes even crazy news sells under the adage that "bad publicity is good publicity," yet there has to be a responsible limit to how much of one's personal life they can share with the public. The fact that a potential dating prospect or mate has access to a social media video highlight, post, or reel of a woman having a tantrum and, worse, ranting and recording the emotional venting session about her ex for her followers or the whole world to see, is tragic. This expectedly may lead the new prospective man in her life to instinctively ponder if dating her would be too risky and volatile for him. Suppose a man observes a woman's temperament and disposition as someone who easily lashes out publicly about private matters, irrespective of the circumstances relating to her valid or invalid feelings. In that case, most men will hesitate to move forward with her due to her lack of confidentiality and couth in handling private matters.

Although venting online may offer some form of temporary or even euphoric relief, the long-term consequences can be damaging. Publicly sharing private relationship struggles may provide a sense of validation or support at the moment. In reality, it can make healing and moving forward so much harder and almost impossible if care isn't taken. In the social media world, we all leave carbon footprints on how we conduct ourselves online and what we choose to post. Our past will come back again to bite us. Nothing on social media, even when deleted, is never really gone forever, and what you posted in an impromptu moment of frustration, pain, hurt, betrayal, vindictiveness, sadness, and anger can retrospectively, in fact, result in perpetual pain that will exist long after the fleeting storm has passed when that post or video resurfaces long after.

In the end, some things are best handled privately and maturely, with the right support system beside you and around you, rather than on a public stage or social media platform, where the power of a screenshot, screen recording, or post 'reshare' can ultimately come back and bite you when you have long since removed yourself from that temporal chapter in your life.

Online Dating Relationship Advice

The disastrous challenge with social media regarding relationships is that people who genuinely need guidance often struggle to find the correct information and resources. When on social media, they often look in the wrong place. Not all advice is helpful, vetted, accurate, researched, and verified. Sadly, social media does not have the tools and algorithm gauges to examine and scrutinize the ample amount of relationship data offered to the public. Some endless posts and opinions are widely misleading in their purpose and perspectives and, unfortunately, are free to circulate on social media platforms for anyone and everyone to digest. While countless content creators offer guidance on the tools for healing from heartbreak or identifying relationship pitfalls, these discussions rarely address the root of the problem, which, in the end, is our individual mental and emotional well-being.

For instance, common phrases like "red flags" and "our highest good" dominate online discussions about relationships. The term 'red flag' is meant to warn about potential relationship issues. However, suppose we recognize these signs yet choose to proceed with the relationship. In that case, we must question our discernment abilities and decision-making processes or skills. At that point, the issue is no longer just about the other person—but, instead, why we sought to ignore the warning signs observed in the first place.

It has been said that those who often blame others feel automatically justified in their beliefs, viewpoints, and their perspectives. However, this is far from the truth. Those crying foul are usually responsible for the damage, harm, or relationship irretrievability. The reality is simple: *truth is often found somewhere between what she says and what he says.* Relationships are rarely one-sided, and there are always multiple perspectives to consider under the notion of the totality of the circumstances.

Moreover, refusing to meet a partner's emotional, material, or physical needs when having the means or previously promising to do so creates space for problems. If that person eventually seeks fulfillment elsewhere, can one say it is their fault entirely? Relationships require mutual assent and reciprocity, and unmet needs often become the root of discontent and the destruction of that relationship's initial foundation.

Another revealing dynamic is when couples eagerly *broadcast* their failed relationships in any form on public forums or virtual platforms. Such behavior is very telling, speaks volumes, and says just as much—if not more—about the person choosing to use the public as a venting conduit or stage as it does about their former partner or the one who allegedly has harmed them. Let's think about this for a moment: When you first started the relationship, *did you invite the public to help you decide whether you should enter that relationship? Was the public involved in your love life or sex life when things were good?* Why do you involve the world to showcase its bitter ending?

Instead, mature relationships are built on the stilts and foundations of accountability and self-reflection, not public validations or social media spectacles.

Hence, this suggests that something deeper within us needs attention, as poor relationship choices often stem from unresolved emotional traumas and wounds, which occurred long before the unveiling of the current relationship challenges and issues at hand. For example, a woman who grew up in a household with a dysfunctional or abusive father is more likely to tolerate similar behavior from a partner or spouse, especially if that partner provides an excuse or momentary validation.

When unhealthy patterns from childhood remain unexamined, they can shape the way we accept and rationalize mistreatment in adult relationships.

Recognizing red flags is only half the battle. The real work lies in understanding why we overlook them and addressing the emotional wounds that make us more likely to tolerate them in the first place.

Similarly, the phrase "our highest good" can be misleading. It implies self-interest rather than mutual benefit. Suppose we expect a partner to meet our highest good. In that case, we may unknowingly place them in an unfair and unjustifiable performance-driven role rather than fostering a genuine relationship based on mutual growth, understanding, and love. The truth is that no relationship is perfect—but a growing relationship is possible.

Although attraction and romance play a crucial role in the beginning stages of love, successful long-term relationships are built on accepting both personalities, shared values, and strong communication—and not just pleasure and society's desires and ideas of romance.

Instead of endless and cyclical trials and errors, narrowing potential matches to '5' distinct types of men is helpful. From this selection, finding the 'one' thus becomes a more transparent and intentional process. Love should not be a matter of luck but a journey of self-discovery, legitimate connections, and personal growth.

Traditionally, relationships have been defined solely by the ideas of love, longevity, and fulfillment. While these elements remain essential, modern relationships require a broader perspective that acknowledges the social and economic realities shaping today's dating environment.

At the heart of this book is the journey to finding the right partner, which begins with self. Since our emotional makeup and past experiences shape how we view relationships, we must align our perspectives. Emotional patterns and emotional maps often influence how we love, trust, and connect with others. Recognizing these emotional foundations is critical to building a healthy and lasting relationship.

The struggle to find true love is not simply a matter of meeting the right person. And if that were the case, relationship disputes wouldn't exist. However, in many cases, the real problem lies within—unhealed wounds from our past experiences, traumas, and dysfunctional behavioral patterns that continue to affect our future choices in choosing partners. It is not uncommon for someone who has faced heartbreak in adulthood to realize that their pain started long before their first romantic relationship. Unresolved wounds, commonly known as "abandonment or avoidant" issues, shape how we approach love and commitment.

Intimacy

The fear of intimacy or 'emotional intimacy' does not just appear in a relationship. Women who struggle with intimacy, especially if it leads to premature breakups, should look a little deeper into their past experiences. This is part of the hard work that honestly and introspectively needs to be done. But without this work being done, keeping a partner won't work. To be clear, intimacy or the idea of intimacy should not be confused with the social slang casually used when one is referring to their having sex with someone. Yet, most times, the term 'intimate,' when used in physical sex discussions, is being misused to explain the physical occurrence between two people. Yes, it is true that when two people engage in the physical act of sex, it is deemed a form of physical intimacy. Yet, it doesn't encompass the notion of or what the term intimacy represents, which consists of several prongs and factors in the relationship between two people. Thereby, being physically intimate with someone includes sex, but having sex with someone doesn't automatically or presumptively equate to a person being emotionally intimate. Physical intimacy is outwardly expressed through touch and sensation, while emotional intimacy is inwardly experienced and felt. It is that feeling of connectedness or togetherness with a partner. The feeling of being one or oneness. It is, therefore, essential to learn and differentiate the two (physical and emotional) intimacy since men and women in relationships may struggle to balance the two levels of intimacy and are likely to emphasize one over the other, creating an imbalance.

Historically, the word *intimacy* [1]is derived from the Latin term *intimus*, meaning "the innermost" or "the core of something." It signifies a deep, internal connection that goes beyond surface-level interactions. When we romanticize *intimus*, we arrive at the word *intimate*—which describes two people sharing a profound bond, striving to know each other inside and out.

Intimacy forms the basis for meaningful relationships, allowing individuals to connect emotionally, physically, intellectually, and spiritually. It fosters trust, understanding, and vulnerability, making it vital to any healthy and lasting relationship. Without intimacy, bonds remain shallow, lacking the depth needed to sustain true companionship.

Sex is a 'form 'of or type of physical intimacy where two bodies share a bond. However, a common misconception among women is the belief that when having sex with a man, they are ultimately *giving* a man sex or *doing him a favor*. This

---

[1] The noun intimacy comes from the Latin word intimare, which means "impress," or "make familiar," which comes from the Latin intimus, meaning "inmost." Intimacy is a close, family-like connection. There is another kind of intimacy — physical intimacy, which comes from having a sexual relationship, which, one hopes, fosters the other kind of intimacy as well.

mindset distorts the true nature of intimacy, either physical or emotional. It conjures a burdensome and obligatory perspective on the sexual act that should be mutually and openly expected and enjoyed by both parties involved. Suppose a woman feels that she must give sex rather than share it. In that case, intimacy is absent, and the innate prowess expected from a woman becomes futile and non-existent. True intimacy stems from a deep emotional connection—and it should never feel like a chore or an obligation.

The same principle applies to men. A man's desire for sex should not be solely for physical gratification but to deepen his intimate and emotional bond with his partner. When emotional intimacy is missing, what merely remains is only physical pleasure—no different from self-indulgence, most referred to as masturbation. Thus, begging one to question, if both men and women are using sex and physical intimacy as a means to an end or obligatory or self-indulgent tools in their interaction with each other, then why is there a need for a relationship?

It also happens that some women sometimes engage in sex with men they are not truly in love with. Over time, such relationships inevitably break down. Suppose a woman is not emotionally drawn to a man. In that case, pretense can only last for so long before the truth reveals itself. In relationships, the phrase *"fake it till you make it"* simply does not work and will not work.

This is why self-reflection and healing are crucial in finding the right partner. Somewhere along the way, society suggested that giving men sex would keep them from leaving a relationship. Although we now know that this rarely works, many women, believing this narrative, sought to engage in sex as a means of *keeping* a man—consequently, transitioning into a performance-based role rather than one rooted in genuine connection, mutual love, or emotional intimacy.

Later in this book, we'll explore why choosing a partner you are genuinely attracted to fosters a natural desire for physical intimacy—one that isn't driven by external pressures, societal ideologies, or familial obligations. When a woman emotionally connects to a man, intimacy will flow organically.

Before placing blame on external circumstances on failed relationships, it's essential to look inward. Taking the time to heal from past emotional wounds will lead to healthier, more fulfilling connections built on strength, self-awareness, and mutual respect rather than unresolved pain.

This is especially important because if a woman's past relationship was based on *performance*—where sex was used as a tool to maintain the relationship—she may struggle to accept a man who doesn't view physical intimacy the same way that she has understood it to mean. And yes, many men value and welcome the *entire* package of emotional and physical intimacy.

Let's consider men with significant responsibilities—leaders, business owners, or those managing organizations. Their demanding schedules may prevent them from prioritizing physical intimacy as often as other men. Their added responsibilities can even affect their physical ability or desire for frequent physical intimacy. However, this does not mean they love or value their partner any less.

Real intimacy is not about obligation, it is about *connection*. And that connection, when genuine, requires emotional and physical alignment in conjunction.

Another major shift in relationships is how they are perceived through cultural lenses. It's surprising how often people judge others without considering their cultural heritage and the societal changes that have shaped their views. In reality, cultural shifts have dramatically altered how relationships function—especially for older women who grew up with more traditional expectations.

The classic model of a man as the sole provider and a woman as a homemaker is no longer the standard for most middle- and lower-class families. The rising cost of living has made financial partnerships a necessity rather than an option. While some couples still embrace a traditional dynamic, particularly those with financial security or a thriving business, this is now a *personal choice* rather than a universal expectation.

Because of this, women must consider the financial aspect of relationships just as seriously as emotional and personal compatibility. Yes, love and intimacy are essential, but basic needs such as food, clothing, and shelter—must also be met. Passion alone does not sustain a relationship; practical considerations are vital for long-term stability and sustainability.

Another major shift is in how the idea of 'attraction' works. The old saying, "looks can be deceiving," has evolved into "looks are deceiving." With the rise of plastic surgery, cosmetic enhancements, and digital filters, appearances can be drastically altered, contemporarily in both men and women. In many cases, it takes time to truly see a person for whom they are beyond their carefully curated image, often at times portrayed or purported on social media, dating apps, or professional platforms.

This may sound harsh, but before you hold my feet to the fire, let me explain. Men are naturally drawn to a woman's authentic beauty. While they may appreciate a polished look, they are not necessarily captivated by enhancements alone. There is nothing wrong with makeup, trendy fashion, or how women present themselves. Still, it's essential to recognize who is genuinely noticing those details. If women pay close attention, they'll realize that most of their compliments about their hair, shoes, and outfits come from other women, not men.

Men, on the other hand, are more reserved when it comes to giving excessive compliments on a woman's appearance, especially in public. In many cases, if a man frequently commented on a woman's outfit, makeup, or accessories, it could be perceived as intrusive or even inappropriate. Because of this, men often hold back, even if they appreciate a woman's style.

However, when a man is genuinely interested in a woman, what matters to him is how she looks naturally—when she wakes up, when she's fresh out of the shower, or when she's most relaxed. That's the version of her he wants to connect with, not just the carefully presented version meant for the world to see. He wants what no other man can access and what no other man is privy to behind closed doors.

Yet, whether indoors or outdoors, time evolution and lifestyle expectations have changed. What was once seen as a romanticized adventure—such as living out of a van—no longer aligns with most people's long-term goals. Stability, personal growth, and shared values have become more critical than ever when choosing a partner. Women today must navigate these evolving dynamics while making decisions that align with their emotional and practical needs, not just spur-of-the-moment, frivolous, spontaneous, or romanticized notions that may once have been afforded to them in their youth's freedoms, naivety, and innocence. Gone are those days.

Challenging Assumptions About Attraction

Some of the ideas in this book may challenge some common beliefs, but they are essential for women to grasp. One key factor in dating is high-value status—the qualities that naturally draw women to certain men. Often referred to in some circles as hypergamy, women are instinctively attracted to men who exhibit confidence, success, strength, and social influence. This preference is not new; it has influenced female partner selection throughout history.

The idea of *marrying up, dating, or pursuing a relationship with a partner with* the most resources rarely leads to lasting fulfillment. Women who engage in this strategy often find themselves facing disappointment.

One reason is that this approach typically requires *monkey branching*—jumping from one relationship to another in search of a better option. In the process, women may leave genuinely good men behind, lured by the *possibility* of finding someone with more status or wealth. However, the truth is, *the grass isn't greener on the other side—it's just watered differently.*

You see, some successful men have built their fortunes *without* a woman involved along the way. Justifiably, they are unlikely to welcome a relationship with open arms that may impede, stagnate, distract, or usurp what they have solely accomplished over time. This causes them to approach dating with skepticism, questioning whether the woman's interest is in *them* or their net worth, monetary assets, or business acumen. Actual, lasting relationships are built on genuine connection, not calculated social climbing and ulterior motives.

However, misconceptions about what makes a man desirable often lead to frustration—both for men and women. Many successful men reflect on their younger years and recall when they weren't the most popular, athletic, or physically attractive. Suppose they experienced rejection from women during their school years. In that case, they may internalize the belief that dating will always be challenging.

Some men assume their chances of securing a fulfilling relationship remain slim without wealth, status, or exceptional looks. They carry this mindset into adulthood, believing that attraction is strictly tied solely to external factors.

But is attraction truly that measurable and predictable?

The reality is more complex. While superficial traits may influence initial attraction, relationships are built on deeper qualities, confidence, emotional intelligence, ambition, and the ability to form genuine connections.

To illustrate this, consider Brandon. In middle school, he was an intelligent student from a modest family. His parents couldn't afford the latest fashion trends, so he wore practical but unbranded clothing. He was passionate about science, excelling in STEM (Science, Technology, Engineering, and Math) subjects, earning recognition as an honor student. Unlike the popular kids at school who customarily participated in sports and social events, Brandon instead spent most of his time studying and had few close friends.

Despite the challenges, he remained focused on his studies. He graduated high school with near-perfect grades and was accepted into an Ivy League college, where he pursued a medical degree. Years later, after completing medical school and his residency, he returned to his hometown to work at the local hospital, eager to give back to the community that raised him. He is now a well-respected doctor, sought after for his expertise and dedication to the medical profession and his patients.

One day, he is assigned to a patient named Ann, who has been admitted for a routine checkup. As he walks into the room, he immediately recognizes her.

"Ann, how are you? It's been so long," he greets her warmly.

"Oh, my goodness. Doctor Brandon? Brandon Wilson from middle school?" she asks rhetorically, but clearly surprised.

"Yes, It's me. How have you been?" he responds warmly, genuinely happy running into an old schoolmate from childhood.

Ann avoids direct eye contact with Brandon, not out of sheer embarrassment from being his patient but rather from the unexpectedness of the surprise. The once shy and unassuming Brandon with thick soda bottle glasses, pen ink stains on his clothing, and being meeker than a mouse ... is now standing before her with a lab jacket on, clipboard in hand, taller than she could have ever imagined, extremely handsome, confident, composed and, obviously very successful.

"How is your family?" she asks him.

"Oh, my parents are doing well and still live on the same street. Thanks so much for asking," he replies.

"No, I meant if you had any immediate family. Are you married with kids?" Ann clarifies.

"Oh, that type of family. No, I'm actually very single at the moment. Lord knows I haven't had the time to date yet, between work, patients, and catching up on doctor notes," he chuckled earnestly.

Ann looks up in disbelief because he would be nuts not to be dating. After all, if you ask her, he looks and sounds like such an amazing catch. Instead, she quietly nods at Brandon as if to agree with what he is saying while concurrently trying to wrap her brain around the fact that this was the same kid who was on the honor roll, who used to sit in the front row of every class and who played in the school's marching band.

Sheepishly, changing the subject, Ann coyly asks Brandon, "Do you remember Roy Mikołaj?" she asks, curious about how much Brandon remembered from their middle and high school days.

"Oh yeah, Roy Mikołaj, Our town's football star. How could I forget? Wait, is he your husband?" Brandon asked, smiling in awe.

"Yes, we got married right after high school," she answers, watching his reaction while simultaneously wrestling with the sudden embarrassment growing inside her as she shares her story and the decisions she made as a young girl in the past.

"Wow, Good for you. What a catch! I'm happy for you guys. I remember that Roy was the most popular guy in school. He was tall, our homecoming king, had perfect hair, and not to mention the school's star athlete," Brandon reminds Ann amiably while reassuring himself that everything has turned out how it was supposed to.

Brandon was nothing like Roy in middle and high school, and most girls never looked his way back then. But he also knew he was where he was supposed to be at the exact place in his life and is grateful for the reminder of how much he has achieved over the years.

Ann, on the other hand, below the surface, wrestles with the internal turmoil and dissonance raging behind her cool, collected, polished, and poised demeanor. Regardless of being the homecoming queen, one of the most beautiful girls in school, and marrying the town's star athlete, she isn't sure that Brandon fully grasps the reality of what her life has turned out to be or instead didn't turn out to be

Her life and marriage to Roy, their five kids, their outdated mini-van, and being a self-proclaimed trophy wife have faced many struggles, and they are barely getting by financially.

"I mean, we were high school sweethearts, but you best believe that we've had our fair share of challenges. I wish I had gone to college like you did—maybe I would have ended up marrying a doctor instead," she says cynically, with an underlying hint of remorse.

"Well, look on the bright side; you're married to the most popular guy in school and pretty much our whole town." Brandon quips goodheartedly, sensing but ignoring the less-than-subtle suggestions, innuendos, and undertones in her melancholic statements.

"Yeah, but not as great as your life turned out," she emphasizes, shifting somewhat provocatively while on the examination table.

"Oh no, Ann, my life wasn't easy. Trust me, I spent years buried in books, surviving on student loans, and sacrificing any semblance of social life to get through medical school and my residency," Brandon admits.

"But it all paid off, right?" she fervently encourages.

"In some ways, yes. But in others, not really. I've always wished I could have been the popular kid in high school, too. Let's be honest: Roy had everything I ever wanted back then. But life doesn't always go the way we imagine or plan, I guess." Brandon reflects.

This short example helps to illustrate and exemplify the different paths that Brandon and Roy chose to take in life as two men.

Roy was the attractive, athletic, and confident young man many girls admired in school. Ann chose him as her life partner, not knowing the future. Meanwhile, Brandon, who once felt overlooked, pursued his strengths and became a successful, hardworking doctor.

Years later, Roy and Ann faced financial hardships, and Ann wondered what life would have been like had she chosen a different path.

Brandon, too, has his reflections, acknowledging that while he has built a successful career, he has also made sacrifices along the way in his personal and familial life.

This short fictional story and illustration teaches us that external qualities like status, good looks, and success can enhance attraction. Still, they do not guarantee a perfect life or relationship for anyone. Attraction is complex and ever-evolving, and beauty is truly in the eye of the beholder, as the old saying goes. The exterior or physical qualities that may have seemed so important at one stage in life may not prove true later in life.

Grasping these dynamics allows men and women to approach relationships with greater clarity and confidence, which requires them to dig a little deeper. A fulfilling partnership is not just about external factors and looks but also about emotional connection, compatibility, and shared values. By shifting focus from outdated expectations to a more realistic perception of modern relationships, men and women can create meaningful, lasting connections.

Why are Men Hesitant to Commit

Women often look for partners who bring value to their lives in different ways—not just financially. However, with constant conversations about high expectations, stories of painful breakups, bitter divorces, and custody battles, many men have begun to question whether pursuing relationships is genuinely worth the effort. They worry they may not meet the standards women seem to expect and, as a result, feel discouraged about dating and any form of commitment.

This hesitation is completely understandable. Dating is not always found on equal playing fields for men and women. Men are expected to make the first move, which means they face more instances of rejection in the early stages of dating. On the other hand, women tend to be the ones who decide to end relationships, meaning men also experience rejection at the end of their relationship or union. This cycle of being turned down when approaching women and potentially facing heartbreaks later—makes dating feel like a high-risk, low-reward experience for many men, thus analogous and no different to the idea and concept of Russian Roulette.

Psychologically, the human brain still retains a primitive side—one we often overlook in modern discussions. While we acknowledge its existence, we take this aspect for granted, perhaps because our ability to multitask and rely on automatic responses has been normalized as expected by human behavior. Reflexes, instincts, and involuntary reactions have all been bundled into the background of our daily lives, rarely examined with the weight they deserve.

Men, in particular, are biologically wired for procreation. In nature, anything unpleasant is naturally avoided—this is part of our built-in survival mechanism. Mating, at its most basic level, is about continuing the species. For humans, this primal drive to procreate still lingers beneath the surface, similar to animals, though layered with social and emotional complexities.

When a man desires a woman sexually, it often stems from both the primal urge to reproduce and the pursuit of pleasure. This dual motivation is important to understand—especially in the context of rejection. When a woman declines physical intimacy, it can trigger a compounded response in a man, activating not only the disappointment of denied pleasure but also the deeper, instinctual drive to mate. This dual rejection can feel magnified, leading to emotional discomfort that some men are unequipped to process maturely.

For immature men, such rejection can feel deeply personal. In some cases, it may even lead them to withdraw from intimacy altogether. To better understand how men internalize rejection—particularly in the early stages of a relationship—it can be helpful to compare it to a financial investment. While the metaphor may not capture the full emotional nuance of relationships, it offers a useful framework: when a man invests emotionally and physically, rejection can feel like a loss, not just of connection, but of value and effort.

Suppose dating was treated and measured like a financial or business investment. In that case, a man's reluctance might begin to seem more and more logical. If we're being honest, it is not far-fetched to admit or believe that most people wouldn't want to continue financially investing in something that promises more losses than ROIs (return on investments) and/or gains. But to be fair, relationships aren't just about risk; they're about connection, companionship, and shared experiences; thus, applying a mere fiscal analysis to what is meant to be an emotional and physical one, would be futile in application.

Viewing love as a transaction misses the deeper emotional and personal fulfillment relationships bring. However, investments pay off over time through the power and concept of 'compound interest, which allows an initial principal amount or 'seed money' to grow exponentially over time. So, imagine someone in their early twenties who made the intellectual and intentional decision to begin investing for their retirement at such a young age. With this investment schedule and plan, by the time they reach their retirement age, their initial or 'principal' investment will have multiplied significantly due to decades of compounding interest.

On the other hand, consider someone in their sixties (not twenties) making the same 'principal' investment, hoping for a similar ROI or compounded interest. Unfortunately, that person in their sixties' principal investment will 'not' grow as much because there isn't enough time for 'compounding' to take effect and have the same results, as we saw in the former example. Ultimately, investing in growth requires time, and when time is not on your side, the potential for long-term returns can prove very limited or even non-existent.

Using the two examples above, we saw that a lump sum investment at an early age paid off well in the former case because a 30-year cushion provides ample time for a significant return. Conversely, in analyzing the latter example, we saw that even the same lump sum investment amount for someone closer to retiring did not yield the same results, as the critical period needed for compounding to maximize returns proved insufficient in the end.

In essence, time is truly an ally when used wisely. Still, it can similarly work against you if you continually miss out on viable opportunities. The sooner you financially invest, the more time your money will have to grow, making early action a key factor in building long-term wealth.

Understanding men may help to relate their way of thinking about relationships to how they steer and maintain their financial investments. Men are often eager to marry and start a family when they are younger. Still, in many cases, they are not fully prepared for the realities of life, the onset of familial obligations, and navigating the choppy waters of relationships, specifically marriage.

Emotional maturity in men tends to develop much more later than in women, which increases the likelihood of making significant mistakes in relationships during their youthful years. This lack of maturity can lead to poor decision-making, misunderstandings, and an inability to handle responsibilities effectively. As a result, many relationships and marriages suffer, ultimately leading to broken homes where the mother becomes the primary caregiver and head of the household.

Their perspective on commitment often shapes men's initial reaction to failed relationships. In their minds, as already mentioned, men equate marriage and long-term relationships to a financial investment and undertaking—one that requires time, effort, and resources.

When a relationship fails, a man may feel like he has lost his investment, much like a financial loss. He may reflect on the years spent, sacrifices, and emotional energy invested. Suppose the outcome is not what he expected. In that case, it can lead to frustration, resentment, or even withdrawal from future commitments with other women.

This mindset is one reason why some men become hesitant to re-enter serious relationships, especially after a painful breakup or divorce. Like in a horrible financial investment, a relationship loss can make men more cautious, skeptical, or unwilling to take another risk. They may start questioning whether long-term commitments are worth the potential downside and whether they should invest in love again.

Men often enter relationships and marriages expecting their commitment to pay off in the long run. Their mindset is built around the belief that no matter what challenges arise, staying dedicated to their spouse will be enough to hold the relationship together and prevent divorce.

Because of this belief, many men are blindsided when faced with separation or divorce. What they may perceive as a simple misunderstanding, a temporary conflict, or just a difference in opinion may be something far more serious, often a breaking point for their partner in the marriage or committed relationship.

Unfortunately, men often realize the gravity of the situation when it's too late to resolve the issue with their partner or spouse. What the man thought was merely a rough and temporal patch in the relationship proves to be a death sentence to their once family unit or proverbial investment. This sudden shift, abrupt change, and permanent loss can leave the man confused, betrayed, and struggling to understand how things unraveled so quickly.

Although, divorce, for many men, feels like a death without a grave—a profound loss with no closure. The truth is that women usually send distress signals when things are not okay in the relationship. When these signals go unnoticed, unacknowledged, or unaddressed, a split becomes inevitable or seems to be in a woman's mind as the only viable and feasible option for the two.

Beyond the emotional toll, society often and unfairly places the blame of failed marriage squarely and primarily on the man, thus holding him accountable for failing to fulfill the roles of husband and father perfectly. In some cases, they may only be granted minimal custody over their children or even lose their parental rights after court orders. In other cases, they may be enthralled in bitter legal battles over assets, alimony, and child support that drag on for years in divorce and family courts.

While men find themselves at fault for some of the regretful decisions made in their relationships and marriages, the aftermath often feels like a life sentence—and the punishment doesn't always fit the crime. The ensuing aftermath often creates a long and punishing ordeal that reshapes the men's lives in unexpected ways.

Albeit this is not to excuse the men's various actions or behaviors that may have led to the breakup, it sheds light on why many men today are hesitant, if not terrified, about the concept of marriage and the long-term commitment required of them. Marriage has become a contractual commitment without guarantees, perks, promises, and securities. At its core, it lacks any rewards for men, not even the rights to their children, if it fails.

A better way to understand a man's pain after a breakup or divorce is by observing how he moves forward. Generally, men tend to lose interest in long-term relationships and marriage and opt for non-committal and fleeting 'situations.' At the same time, women are more likely to seek another committed relationship almost immediately. Why is this the case? Because women process the pain and discouragement of a failing relationship while still in it

When a woman expresses dissatisfaction in her relationship or marriage, she often seeks solutions, hoping to fix the relationship before making final decisions. However, during this time, she also begins the process of emotional detachment.

Men, on the other hand, are often slower to catch on. Many don't realize the depth of their partner's unhappiness until it's too late. While the woman has been emotionally preparing to leave, the man is still under the assumption that things will work out. When he finally recognizes the seriousness of the situation, the emotional distance is already too great to bridge. Thus, the infamous concept of a couple or a marriage being "irretrievably broken" comes to life.

This delayed reaction is why breakups and divorces hit men differently. By the time a woman walks away and leaves, she has already mourned the relationship and the closing of the curtains. However, the pain is fresh and unexpected for the man, making it much harder for him to grasp, process, and move forward. This is why many men hesitate to re-enter long-term commitments—they associate relationships with emotional blind spots and painful losses that they never saw coming.

When a breakup happens, men process the loss of the relationship in a way that often leaves them with unanswered questions. They replay events in their minds, wondering if there was something they could have done differently, but by the time they start asking these questions, it's already too late. That emotional wound becomes deeply tied to the type of relationship where the breakup occurred.

If it was a marriage, they may avoid marriage in the future because of the trauma. They may steer clear of serious commitments if it is a long-term relationship. This is where the term "commitment issues" comes into play—it's not always about an inherent fear of commitment, but rather an avoidance of the pain and loss associated with it due to previous lived experiences for the man.

Younger men are highly observant of this phenomenon. Unfortunately, they have listened to older men who have experienced failed relationships, difficult breakups, and the financial hardships that often followed their divorces. The pain and resentment expressed by older men sadly has become a cautionary tale for the next generation, advertently and inadvertently shaping their views on relationships. Furthermore, before society catches up with the trend, women notice that men have become avoidants. The present high levels of men avoiding long-term commitment can be directly attributed to painful losses they encountered in their previous relationships.

This creates a chain reaction—a psychological phenomenon known as groupthink, where a collective belief spreads, influencing individual decisions. Social media further amplifies this mindset, exposing men to endless discussions about divorce horror stories, unfair, egregious alimony settlements, child custody nightmares, and heartbreaks. Even though these narratives often lack balance, they serve as a strong and disastrous deterrent for men seeking relationships, making them hesitant to pursue them, especially in marriage.

While we all know there are two sides to every story, social media often presents only one side, reinforcing fear and skepticism. This overwhelming wave of negative experiences discourages many men from even considering marriage or serious commitment, even when their personal circumstances might be different.

Women must understand that men whom a breakup has hurt may not be emotionally ready or fully healed to enter a new relationship. The pain from a past failed relationship can create deep-seated and genuine fears, making them hesitant to commit again, irrespective of a new woman trying to come into their life who may very well check off all the boxes.

Moreover, the misguided and unfounded societal narrative that *women* are often responsible for wrecking good relationships—while men are portrayed as having done nothing wrong—only reinforces existing fears and frustrations. What makes this even more complex is that this message is now amplified by *women influencers* on social media. It leads one to ask, "What happened to sisterhood?"

As a result, many men feel *vindicated* in believing they weren't at fault for past breakups or inevitable divorces. This shift in perspective—championed by women who openly share secrets about female intent, strategies, behavior, or 'misbehavior'—hasn't necessarily encouraged men to pursue healthier relationships, either. Instead, it has only given many men further justifications for their walking away altogether.

While some content creators may be solely financially motivated, the reality is that some of their messages undoubtedly resonate with men. Whether these perspectives are entirely accurate or not, they subsequently shape the modern dating culture in ways that make men increasingly hesitant to commit.

It is actually very confusing for men to hear women, either online on the various social media platforms available, taking the time out to advise them on ways to watch out for toxic women and, in some cases, even further discouraging men from dating altogether. This shift highlights how much social media is shaping modern relationships. It is no longer just men warning each other about commitment risks. Now, women themselves are cautioning men against getting involved in relationships with other toxic and pariah-like women.

Consequently, this creates a new challenge in the dating market, where trust is being eroded from both sides. Suppose men are already reluctant to commit due to past experiences, and now women are also discouraging them from engaging in relationships with women. In that case, it raises an important question: How do men and women bridge the growing divide in modern dating?

So, what happens to men after a painful breakup? Many of them focus on improving their financial lives and fiscal positioning in society as men. What changes in men as they mature and heal from divorces and breakups lies in their ability to prioritize key objectives. For example, it is more important for men to have financial stability rather than chasing vanity and popularity.

If their past relationships caused financial losses, they will likely focus on creating or re-creating their wealth. Some of them become workaholics. They also learn from the mistakes made through their lived experiences. So, when mature men approach dating, they are very cautious. They seek a reciprocal commitment and not pleasure.

Going back to the investment approach highlighted earlier, if you lose money in the stock market, you'll be more careful the next time or may never reinvest. The sad news in relationships is that most men quit relationships and marriages altogether. They settle for having a friend with benefits if they can find one. Some even travel to foreign countries, hoping a partner from a different culture would better suit them.

Then, other kinds of men take accountability for their mistakes and are willing to make necessary adjustments to begin dating and even getting married. The point here is to recognize how men experience pain because whether we like it or not, most men available for relationships have either experienced personal loss or pain from a broken relationship. Unlike women, men are not eager to enter long-term commitments or marriages.

It is also important to understand that men naturally have a hunter's mindset when dating. When they see an attractive woman, their instinct is to initiate contact through conversation or a direct invitation to spend time together. While this may not always be an immediate or obvious pursuit, the underlying intent is to explore the possibility of knowing her on a deeper, more personal level.

Women tend to socialize in groups, especially when attending social gatherings. While this fosters a sense of camaraderie and safety, it also makes it increasingly difficult for men to approach one specific woman out of 'that group.'

How does a 'one' man single out 'one' woman from the pack of her other female counterparts to express his interest in the one woman alone? Almost impossible to some, rude, some may say, and indeed very awkward to many.

Approaching a woman alone is much simpler than being surrounded by friends because the latter only interrupts and complicates the natural and intuitive dynamic between a male and female when first meeting. Suppose a group of friends surrounds a woman. In that case, the man fears entering a situation filled with distractions, unsolicited opinions, and meritless judgment from her peers. Alas, the mere possibility of being rejected in front of an audience and the fear of embarrassment or even the possibility of group judgment can understandably make men hesitant to make the first move.

As a result, the traditional idea of men confidently approaching a woman, to which they may be initially drawn or attracted, is facing a new obstacle and modern-day dilemma. With various social norms, unspoken courtesy protocols, and expectations evolving, *How do men navigate this new reality of group interactions while still making genuine connections with women?*

In addition, there's the idea that men only primarily seek out women in order to have sex with them. Although this is true to a certain extent, this is not a generalized conception for all men and really depends on the man's age and stage in life.

A younger man is typically more focused on the thrill of the chase, the excitement of a new relationship, and the validation that comes with attracting a woman. He wants to impress, splurge, and establish himself as desirable. However, he often begins to recognize the importance of being selective when choosing a partner through costly mistakes or painful breakups.

For a mature man, priorities shift. He is more likely to seek a long-term relationship where companionship, emotional stability, and potentially starting a family become more important than fleeting pleasure. At this stage, he is interested in a woman's thoughts, values, and emotional intelligence.

One of the most important qualities a mature man seeks in a woman is her ability to be nurturing. A nurturing woman naturally and inherently contributes to a man's growth and expansion. Just as a business idea similarly requires incubation and care to develop into something successful, so do men who 'are focused on personal and professional growth. A mature man values a woman who can positively impact his ideas, goals, and well-being.

This is why, beyond physical attraction, men at this stage are more interested in how a woman cares, nurtures, and engages with the world around her. Her emotional stability and mental health are just as crucial as her outward appeal because he understands that a strong partnership is built on more than just chemistry—it's about long-term compatibility and support.

For men, caring, in this context, refers to how the woman treats people in various situations and in different environments. For example, on a date, does she express her disappointment over a wrong meal by lashing out at the waiter, or does she handle it gracefully? Does she tip well based on the service received? Does she show appreciation for those working in jobs often considered somewhat entry-level or low-level by society, such as cleaning, serving, grooming, and hospitality?

Mature men will often subtly test a woman's character during a date. One typical example is asking her to leave the tip after a meal—not with her own money, but with his. This isn't about finances; it's about observing her generosity and ability to acknowledge and respect those whose livelihood depends on service.

During courtship and dating, mature men are highly observant. They recognize that long-term relationships require attraction, values, temperament, and compatibility with emotional intelligence. To them, first impressions matter because they offer insights into the future.

For example, an argument during the early stages of a relationship isn't just an isolated disagreement. A mature man will project that argument five years into the future, imagining how much worse it could become if deeper commitments—such as marriage or children—are involved. What may seem like a minor conflict to a woman at the moment could be a deal-breaker for a man who envisions such future turmoil as prospective impediments to his need for peace, a home, and serenity.

It is pertinent for women to grasp that men, especially those seeking long-term commitment, constantly assess their potential love interests. Their decisions about relationships are not just about emotions in the present but about forecasting what life will look like with that person over a period and an elongated amount of time.

Mental health is another important factor in a mature man's selection criteria. These men have lived experiences, made their fair share of mistakes, and, in many cases, have been in long-term relationships or marriages, sometimes with children. Because of this, they tend to prioritize mental and emotional stability in a relationship.

This is not about mental illness but rather emotional self-regulation. A mature man looks for a woman who can manage her emotions, especially when things don't go her way. If she has a bad day or feels overlooked, can she constructively communicate her frustrations, or does she resort to emotional outbursts, public confrontations, or unnecessary drama?

Men today are increasingly cautious about relationships that easily escalate into conflicts or unjustifiably physical altercations, potentially involving law enforcement and the court systems. Through personal experience or observation, many have learned that they often face legal or social consequences in heated situations, regardless of who instigates the conflict. They understand that provocation often plays a role in physical altercations. They are mindful of avoiding relationships where they may be put in situations that challenge their self-control. Thus, they will prevent environments that feel synonymous with entrapment and intentional provocation by their female counterpart.

During the initial dating phase, mature men often observe a woman's behavioral patterns closely, paying attention to potential red flags such as impulsiveness or aggressive tendencies. One common concern is when a woman exhibits a consistently competitive or combative dynamic, particularly in a way that challenges a man's role rather than fostering mutual respect. Phrases or attitudes like *"What you can do, I can do better"* can create tension, as they may be perceived as an attempt to assert dominance rather than build a partnership.

Additionally, while some may assume men are primarily drawn to wealth or material status in a partner, many men—especially those with a strong provider instinct—are more motivated by the opportunity to contribute and support their household. Suppose a man feels that his role as a provider is diminished because his partner significantly out-earns him or has more significant resources. In that case, it can sometimes lead to internal conflict, resentment, inadequacy, and self-emasculation. This dynamic is not necessarily about financial superiority but the traditional masculine drive to contribute meaningfully to a relationship. Without it, men don't know their place in the dynamics of a relationship between a man and a woman.

Additionally, mature men are not interested in competitive relationships. They have already been through those experiences in their younger years or have seen family members or friends endure them. Instead, they seek a relationship where both partners complement each other rather than constantly challenge one another, toxically and volatilely.

Another important factor in men being hesitant is mental health. It is critically important to recognize that mental health facilitates our ability to communicate, comprehend, and much more effectively. We can even say mental health is a gateway to our souls.

How we process information, manage our emotions, and make decisions depends on our ability to think clearly and remain levelheaded. As men mature, they place increasing value on emotional stability and seek a life that is as free from unnecessary stress and conflict as possible. This is often referred to as "Drama-Free Living." The older people get, the more they desire calm and stability in their relationships.

When entering the dating world, it's essential to understand the expectations and dynamics that come with different age groups. A man's priorities, emotional needs, and outlook on relationships evolve based on his life stage and experiences.

For example, a man experiencing a mid-life crisis is often in a self-reflection phase, reassessing his identity, career, and future. During this period, he may focus on finding stability rather than actively pursuing a serious relationship. This can make him emotionally unavailable or hesitant to commit as he still navigates his challenges.

Recognizing these differences can help individuals approach dating with greater awareness, ensuring that expectations align with a partner's life stage and emotional readiness.

To bridge the gap in modern dating, women must reevaluate their preferences and gain clarity on what they truly seek in a partner. It's crucial to recognize that many men may hesitate to commit due to a lack of attraction, personal challenges, and unresolved baggage needing attention.

Women can foster deeper connections and build healthier, more fulfilling partnerships by shifting perspectives and approaching relationships more intentionally. Recognizing that both men and women carry their own experiences and emotional weight allows for more tolerance, compassion, and alignment in dating. In life, we know what we want. Still, we should only take what we can get without manipulating others into giving us what we know they cannot do.

Being ready means healing from past emotional wounds while fully letting go of previous relationships and being willing to embrace the challenges that come with new love. Many women underestimate the impact of unresolved emotions. When painful emotions are not dealt with, they can cloud judgment and create cycles that destructively repeat in current or future relationships.

Additionally, women often focus on why men seem hesitant to commit without considering that men, too, carry emotional baggage. When a relationship ends, the pain does not simply vanish—it often lingers and influences future decisions. Instead of assuming men are unwilling to commit, a more productive approach is to seek clarity on why a particular man may be hesitant. Questions such as, what experiences shaped his fears? Or what past hurts influence his choices? These are all critical questions for a partner to ask.

When women sincerely understand a man's past relationship experiences, dating stops feeling like a game of uncertainty. Instead, it becomes a meaningful journey toward a real connection. Sometimes, the couple may find themselves far apart in their experiences. However, it is excellent to work on themselves together and move closer. Perfection in relationships is found in recognizing that we come from a varied background, but love helps us close that gap.

Good Men, Is it a Myth?

A common question in dating is, *"Where are all the good men?"* But the real issue isn't a lack of men—it's about finding one who is both mature and compatible. If being *good* means a man who is understanding, kind, generous, and loving, then the reality is that he may be closer than many women think.

However, several factors can prevent a woman from recognizing or attracting a good man. A woman dealing with antisocial tendencies or other untreated mental health struggles may have difficulty identifying and appreciating a good man. Her perception of relationships may be clouded, making it difficult to form deep, meaningful connections.

Similarly, suppose a woman carries unhealed wounds from past relationships or struggles with addictions. In that case, she may unknowingly push away the very kind of man she desires. Without proper healing or therapy, she may remain stuck in unhealthy patterns, unable to embrace a stable and loving relationship.

Another challenge arises when other people's opinions easily influence a woman. If she allows external pressures to dictate essential life choices— from those who claim to want *the best for her*—she may overlook a great man standing right before her. The pressure to seek status, wealth, or an idealized romance can cloud her judgment and lead her away from authentic connections.

That being said, women aren't just searching for any partner; they are seeking a man who can offer more than a surface-level connection. Yet, recognizing and attracting a good man requires self-awareness, emotional healing, and clarity on what truly matters in a relationship. When women take the time to reflect on their needs and remove obstacles in their path, they open themselves up to the very kind of love they've always desired.

When we talk about maturity in a man, we mean someone who is emotionally stable, responsible, and committed to a long-term relationship rather than seeking casual flings. A mature man understands the value of commitment and is ready to invest in something meaningful.

Compatibility is just as important. It's about shared interests and how well two people's personalities and values align. A genuinely compatible partner creates balance and harmony in a relationship, making it easier to grow together harmoniously rather than constantly struggling to stay connected.

The challenge for many women isn't a shortage of men but instead finding one who is both emotionally mature and a good fit for them. Shifting the focus from "Where are good men?" to "How do I find a partner who aligns with my values and relationship goals?" can make a big difference in acceptance and approach.

Many women naturally seek men who are strong, financially secure, and attractive. While these qualities are undeniably appealing, they have also contributed to a growing concern among men about their place in the dating market. Many average-income and less conventionally attractive men feel overlooked, questioning whether they stand a fair chance against wealthier or more physically desirable men.

Interestingly, this preference has not been met with enthusiasm from men. Instead, many are bonding together in resistance to this notion. They openly challenge the idea that financial success or physical appearance should be leading presumptions that dictate a man's worth and contributory value in relationships. Men see a flawed and shallow system that elevates high-status men but often leaves them vulnerable to financial loss, emotional distress, and failed relationships. Many men wonder where and how to find the right balance.

Case in point: Nowadays, average men continue to observe how wealthy men lose significant portions of their wealth in divorces after painful breakups. This does not inspire confidence in either group—those who struggle to attract partners and those who seemingly "have it all" ...but ultimately lose it. As a result, both groups are becoming increasingly skeptical of modern dating expectations, leading to a more cautious and even resistant approach to relationships.

Another misconception is the belief that wealthy or high-status men always have access to the best caliber of women. The reality is that merely being a successful man doesn't automatically guarantee or equate to a man experiencing a fulfilling relationship with a woman.

Take celebrities, for example. A famous actor, entertainer, or athlete may struggle to tell whether a woman is genuinely interested in him as a person or if she is drawn to his wealth, status, and fame. Because of this, many high-status men date within their social circles, where they feel their lifestyle is better understood and has already been experienced by the prospective women they come across in this tight-knit and close-knit community of peers.

This helps to explain why Hollywood actors, entertainers, and musicians often form relationships with fellow celebrities rather than seeking partners outside of the entertainment industry.

If attraction and status worked predictably, we would expect to see more women marrying into wealth and power. However, contrary to popular belief, these cases are actually quite rare. Financial success and influence may make a man more desirable, but they don't guarantee true love or a lasting relationship. Many successful men struggle to find meaningful connections, proving that attraction is more complex than money or status.

Where are The Good Men?

Before exploring where good men may be found, it's important to acknowledge that people tend to associate with those with the same mindset. Ask yourself these questions?

What's your favorite pastime activity? What do you do for a living? Who is your best friend(s)?

These questions, much more like them, will most likely point you to where your type of good man can be found. In other words, it is not easy to go looking for relationships in circles you are not familiar with. People's way of life and thinking generally mirrors those they associate and mingle with.

As social beings, we seek connections and belonging. Our thoughts and emotions need an outlet, and social gatherings help fulfill this deep-rooted desire in our being to be part of something collectively bigger than ourselves. Interestingly, this desire for a social connection stems from our childhood.

If we were fortunate enough to grow up in a strong family unit, our early interactions were shaped by the relationships we formed with family members. The larger the family, the more opportunities we had to engage in different social activities, and we learned how to explore relationships through those shared experiences. This foundation doesn't disappear as we age—it continues to influence how we form and maintain relationships.

Studies suggest that 'an only child' is more likely to develop greater independence than children who grow up with multiple siblings. This distinction plays a role in dating. If your partner is an only child, he may exhibit a higher level of self-sufficiency or seem less inclined toward social activities than someone who grew up in a large family where social interaction was a daily norm.

As you'll see later, much of what you do as a woman—your expectations, relationship patterns, and emotional responses—was already instilled in you from a young age. This is why revisiting and reconciling with your early experiences is crucial, as they shape how you approach relationships today. Understanding these influences can provide deeper insight into your dating preferences and help foster healthier connections.

A classic example of this is the story of the holiday ham. Every year, a grandmother would cut both ends off the ham before placing it in the oven. Her daughters continued the tradition, believing it was necessary for even cooking. One day, an argument broke out between them—one thought it helped distribute heat evenly, while the other insisted the ham could be baked as it was

Their mother, noticing the disagreement, suggested asking the grandmother directly. When they did, she explained that she cut both ends off because her pan was too small to fit the whole ham. The entire kitchen burst into laughter.

You see, the truth was always in plain sight, but no one had ever questioned the reasoning behind the tradition.

Similarly, many beliefs women hold about men and relationships come from earlier matriarchal or familial influences. If you grew up hearing your mother, aunts, or other women say things like, "All men are dogs," "All men cheat," "Never trust a man," or "Your father is a deadbeat," these messages may have been embedded and indoctrinated into your subconscious.

Without being able to even question or seek clarity, at such a young age, about what these statements meant or why they were being said, the things that 'the young girl' hears during her childhood become ingrained beliefs. Inherited beliefs, which inadvertently later shape and mold her perception of relationships, often make them more difficult for her than they would have been if not for the unsolicited 'advice' received throughout her childhood and over the years. Thus, understanding where these thoughts originated from and then challenging them becomes necessary. Her intentionally challenging what she once knew or thought she knew can make a difference in a woman's life and help break generational and statistical ideologies and societal and familial beliefs.

So, where are the good men hiding? They aren't hiding—they exist in plain sight, from the most underrated and unexpected spaces to the most exclusive and sophisticated environments. Men typically socialize within their circle of influence, meaning the people they spend time with often reflect their values, mindset, net worth, and lifestyle choices.

In fact, if you were to observe a man's close friends, you could likely predict his influence, income bracket, interests, and general attitude toward relationships. This isn't a matter of prophecy or fortune-telling—it's simply human nature, the appreciation of patterns, and the importance of dynamics. People naturally gravitate toward those who share their values, goals, and ways of thinking.

Good men aren't defined by their financial status, whether wealthy or not. They are 'good men' because their core character and beliefs align with what is generally considered respectable and acceptable in society.

It starts with a simple question: What are you looking for in a man? If marriage is your goal, understand that men who are serious about long-term commitment seek stability. They intentionally surround themselves with social circles in specific environments, which minimize unnecessary drama, provide safety, sustain their peace, and expose them to like-minded colleagues, peers, family men, and associates.

For example, these men are likelier to attend a sporting event than heading out to a bar for a happy hour every Friday night. Why? Because sports events are generally family-friendly, filled with positive energy, and provide a structured social setting. The atmosphere is cheerful, the audience is engaged, and while alcohol may be served, it is typically done with caution—especially since families with children are often present.

Of course, this doesn't mean a good man never goes to a bar or pub. However, if he does, it's usually for a specific reason rather than a regular habit. And when he does go, he likely approaches it differently than someone who predictably and incessantly spends every weekend in that environment.

If you want to meet good men, pay attention to where they choose to spend their time. They prioritize places and activities that align with their values and long-term goals—so if you want to find them, it helps to be in the right places, too.

Depending on their budgets and preferences, good men tend to choose less chaotic environments. If sporting events aren't an option, they might opt for a restaurant, perhaps sitting at the high table for a drink or two. The common theme is that they generally avoid places with a high likelihood of chaos and unnecessary and fruitless interactions.

Business clubs, for instance, are not emphasized here because they are often membership-driven and cater to professional circles for specific interests. However, if a woman seeks a high-value man, joining a local country club or a similar private organization might be a strategic move, as these spaces often attract professionals and established individuals.

The challenge with finding a suitable partner in such an environment as a corporate business club or professional membership club is that men can sense when a woman doesn't truly belong. For example, a golf country club exists for avid golfers, not those looking to network or find a relationship. Both men and women who are genuinely passionate about the sport can easily recognize someone who joins for reasons other than a sincere interest in golf. Similarly, social clubs are designed for people who share common values, professions, or hobbies, making it difficult for outsiders to blend in naturally. This assuredly helps to vet out 'those' with ulterior motives and allows them to wean themselves out from such 'social groups' due to their less than genuine, opportunistic, and conspicuous intentions ... more obvious to the others than they inherently realized. Joining an organization solely to seek a partner can come across as 'thirsty' and largely superficial, which often backfires.

A woman should instead consider developing an authentic interest before joining such clubs. She can achieve this by learning a sport, understanding the culture of a club, or building knowledge in a particular area of business or finance while creating genuine connections rather than forced ones.

For instance, a businessman seeking a partner would naturally be drawn to an entrepreneurial woman who understands his world rather than someone pretending to fit in. Authenticity, curiosity, and shared interests create stronger and more meaningful relationships.

Though sometimes debated, religious organizations can also be a good place to meet men who hold marriage and family values at the core of their beliefs. After all, most religions are fundamentally built on faith and family. However, the key here is authenticity. A woman should never join a gym, a specialty club, or a professional organization to find a man. Doing so without genuine interest in those spaces can be disingenuous, desperate, and manipulative. Relationships built on self-serving motives often lead to disappointment, as inauthenticity becomes evident over time.

The honest answer to where the good men are is that they are everywhere and depend on a woman's values, patience, authenticity, and preferences. To be more intentional about meeting quality men, one must first embody the qualities they hope to attract.

For example, meeting men at night clubs—where intoxication, exposure to unsafe environments, inebriation, possible substance abuse, crime, and sexually provocative behaviors are prevalent—is not necessarily an ideal and foundational place to meet someone interested in a serious, long-term relationship.

No offense, but men typically go to these venues to have fun and let loose, not to find a future wife or 'the one.' While exceptions exist in such environments in finding love, most men do not instinctively look for meaningful relationships in these nightclubs. A man who similarly meets a woman in the nightclub or strip club environment will always carry the negative association or connotation in his mind of where he met her that first time and what she was doing there; if things ever evolve into something more, down the road.

Socially fluid women—those who frequently engage in casual social settings—often discourage men from commitment. Many men associate nightclubs and nightlife with temporary and fleeting escapes rather than a place where serious relationships are born. On the contrary, after a painful breakup, men often visit these kinds of places to drink their pain away, seek distractions, or momentarily reclaim their sense of masculinity through casual and sexual encounters, with no long-term intention or expectations of commitments. If women were to ask adult entertainers, strippers, or dancers working at these venues, they would likely confirm that many male clients are there due to personal struggles, failing marriages, broken relationships, or even addictions.

For a woman to frequent such places in search of a relationship says more about her mindset than the man she meets there. Suppose a relationship with someone from a nightclub setting ends in dysfunction. In that case, blaming the man ignores the accountability of the choices made. While exceptions exist, a serious woman generally would not seek a life partner in these environments—nor would she take a man she meets there seriously unless there was a strong reason to believe otherwise.

The fascination with men considered high status, financially successful, and physically appealing often overlooks an important reality. These men make up only a small percentage of the population.

In the United States, roughly 10% of the population falls into the millionaire category. However, this figure includes both men and women and entire households. When you remove married couples and families from the equation, the percentage of eligible, available, high-status male bachelors shrinks significantly.

What does this tell us? These men are, in fact, rare. Not only that, but they are also highly sought after, giving them an abundance of options for dating. As a result, they are less likely to settle down quickly, which creates a contradiction: many women are drawn to these men because of their status and appeal, yet these very qualities make them more selective and less inclined to commit easily.

This imbalance in supply and demand often leads to unrealistic expectations, where women compete for a small percentage of men who, by virtue of their desirability, may not prioritize exclusivity or long-term commitment.

This is why women need to focus not just on external traits like wealth and looks but also on qualities that lead to a lasting connection. A genuinely fulfilling relationship comes from finding a man who is successful, emotionally available, compatible, and genuinely interested in commitment.

That's where the concept of "Every Woman Has 5 Men to Choose From" comes into play—women have more potential partners than they may realize if they broaden their understanding of what makes for a great relationship.

So, the common belief that men work hard to build wealth and status to provide for others or attract a great partner is false. While this may be true for some, many successful men are driven by personal ambition and a deep passion for their goals. Their achievements in business, sports, or personal development are often a result of relentless dedication and not just a desire for money or relationships.

For these men, financial success is a byproduct of their efforts, not the ultimate goal. Their drive comes from a sense of purpose and accomplishment rather than just pursuing status.

While high value as a trait in men influences attraction, it doesn't mean that only wealthy men find love. A man's ability to connect, communicate, and provide emotional security often matters more in the long run than just his financial standing. While the high-value mindset can shape what a woman seeks in a partner, its real impact is on the men who choose to grow and improve themselves.

A man does not become successful to attract women—he does it for himself. While women may benefit from their success, the real reward belongs to the man who has built his life through hard work, dedication, and self-discipline. His value is not dependent on a relationship, and his success remains his own, no matter who enters or walks out of his life.

Chapter 2

Dating In the Modern World?

Modern dating is, without a doubt, the mother of all confusion. Younger women often hear nostalgic stories about men who once embodied chivalry. Yet, many can hardly say they have personally experienced it.

In today's world, technology and materialism drive relationships, leaving little room for the depth and sincerity that once defined courtship. For mature women, this shift is particularly challenging. Meaningful conversations—once the foundation of emotional connection—are now reduced to abbreviated text messages and emojis, where three simple icons can replace the weight of one's expressed emotions that say, *"I love you."*

Although the level of disconnect and our obsession with 'technology versus touching and agreeing' is entirely mind-boggling, here we are. This is our new reality. A reality where a dating app profile—consisting of little more than a photo and minimal contact information on the profile page—is enough to initiate a sexual encounter masked as a 'genuine interest or connection.' A simple swipe left or right is all it takes to signal, *"Let's meet and have sex."* No words are necessary, and no questions are asked.

It's one thing if people could honestly say that meeting someone on a dating app rarely leads to sex—but let's be real, that's not usually how it plays out, especially with apps that lean more toward hookups than long-term connections. However, what's just as important is how normalized online dating has become—particularly among younger adults. According to a 2023 Pew Research Center survey, 53% of Americans under 30 have used dating apps, and about 20% ended up in a relationship.

While we don't have enough data to say how long these relationships last, we know finding a partner through a dating app is possible. Still, that 20% success rate means only 2 out of 10 people are finding a match that turns into something tangible. That's not nothing, but those odds feel pretty low when it comes to something as profoundly human and essential as love.

We're wired for connection—emotional, spiritual, physical. It's part of what keeps us going. So, if dating apps give us a 1 in 5 chance, it almost sounds like the other 8 out of 10 are being left out in the cold.

So, how many of these dates end up in one-night stands or sex after a few dates? We can say that a majority of online dates do not go anywhere. More than 50% of people surveyed did not even have a positive or a negative opinion of online dating. This is not to say that online dating doesn't work, but it raises an important question. Do we really have to shift from traditional meeting people and getting to know them in our usual social circles?

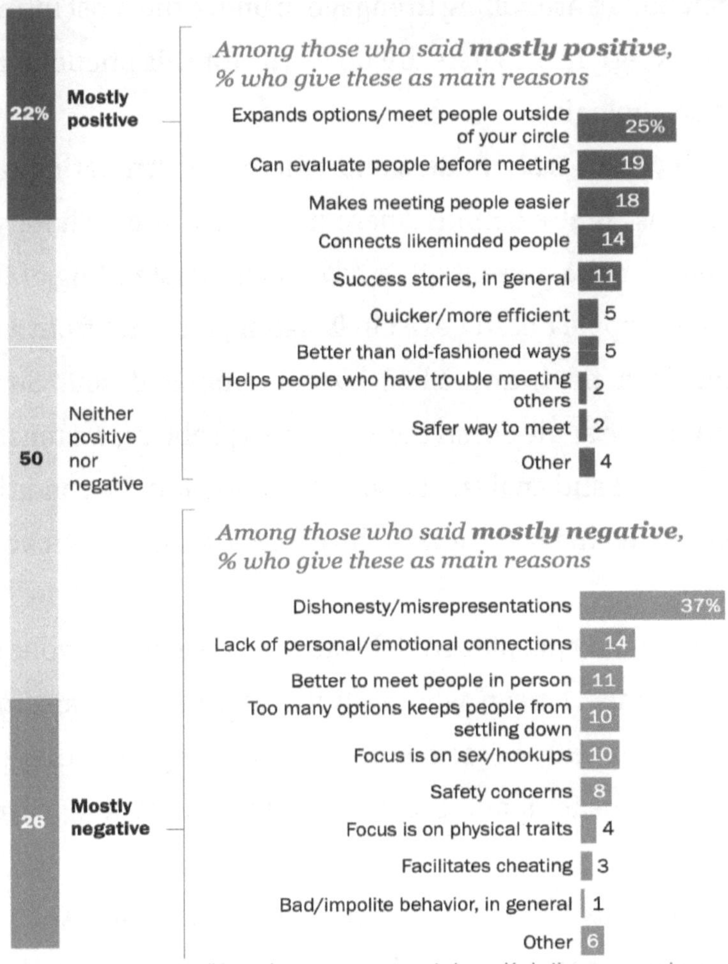

Note: Respondents who did not give an answer are not shown. Verbatim responses have been coded into categories, and figures may add up to more than 100% because multiple responses were allowed.
Source: Survey of U.S. adults conducted Oct. 16-28, 2019.
"The Virtues and Downsides of Online Dating"

PEW RESEARCH CENTER

I won't even attempt to decode the full implications of this other than to say that in these scenarios, two people know nothing about each other beyond their physical appearance—yet their bodies are willing to engage in one of the most intimate human experiences. There are no words for this phenomenon, so I must apologize.

However, to truly understand where modern dating takes us, we must first examine where it took us from. Those who struggle with the present often have no understanding of their past. A bad apple doesn't exist in isolation; it comes from a tree planted in a field, nourished by contaminated soil. Simply discarding the apple doesn't solve the real problem; we must dig a little deeper and analyze the soil, the roots, and the conditions that produced the bad apple in the first place. And this involves work.

Hence, many people avoid the necessary work to invoke life-altering change. I mean, who really wants to see a therapist who unequivocally will seek to tell them many things that they may not like to hear about themselves, their past and current behaviors?

Many of us think that the problem usually lies with our partner and not ourselves, and we wonder why narcissism starts with an elevated ego. A person who always thinks "higher of themselves than they ought to be," or "thinking that whatever the issue happens to be, it is never their fault," or those who are quick to point an accusing finger, and in most cases are the very instigators attempting to shift or project their faults elsewhere. So yeah, this is the work we need to do. It is called introspection. It is called self-re-evaluation.

This chapter will take you back to the foundations of modern dating. By understanding its origins, you can approach relationships with clearer expectations. As a woman, this knowledge will help you recognize serious intentions from men and avoid the fleeting distractions of modern flings.

After all, just like that bad apple, something may look good on the outside—until you sink your teeth into it.

The Origin of Romanticism

Romanticism began in the late 1700s and early 1800s, when industrialization changed our everyday life. Machines replaced traditional manual labor; people found new and more efficient living methods, such as improved food production, better transportation, and innovative work opportunities. This era also challenged existing beliefs, much like social media has done in our times.

In that era, people started emphasizing freedom of expression, questioned established traditional authorities, and shifted the definition of their family life from duty to being driven by the pursuit of happiness and emotional fulfillment.

So, romanticism isn't an ancient view of relationships but a product of industrialization and modern civilization. It emerged when families no longer spent most of their time on manual labor because machines handled much of the work. With more time and energy available, people began to value emotional fulfillment.

During this period, men could no longer prove their worth solely by showing physical strength on the farm, in a factory, or by how much they earned, especially as women became more independent and financially self-reliant. As a result, men had to find new ways to impress their partners, often turning to chivalry—wooing women with gifts and surprises to bring happiness and emotional satisfaction.

During the Enlightenment, people began to value emotions, intuition, and personal experiences over strict logic. In dating, this shift made finding love a personal journey focused on individual happiness rather than duty or commitment to marriage, parents, family, and home. Before this change, families arranged marriages because parents believed they knew what was best for their children. They often sought to marry their daughters into wealthy and influential families for financial security and familial ties.

They preferred hardworking men to help the family weather hard times. Parents carefully selected and vetted potential suitors for their daughters to ensure this. So, the shift in relationships, which emphasized romantic gestures, emotional fulfillment, and happiness, led both men and women to prioritize societal and romantic ideals as the foundation of love.

Simply put, the romantic view of relationships tells people to trust their 'gut feelings' when choosing a partner. It believes true love happens wholly and naturally, without following society's rules or logical thinking. In this view, strong emotions show that the connection is deep and meaningful. People who deeply engage in romantic perspectives often share an everyday bliss; they tend to be overtaken and captivated by passion in each other, and this distinctive trait becomes the basis of their connection. From this perspective, love is meant to flourish without being restricted by social class, family pressures, work duties, or practical concerns. This concept frequently appears in literature, art, and film, where the main characters overcome various obstacles to pursue their love.

While romanticism values strong feelings and personal happiness, it has its drawbacks. Focusing too much on passion can cause people to ignore key parts of a lasting relationship, like compatibility, shared values, and everyday realities. It can also set up unrealistic expectations by suggesting that true love should always be overwhelming.

Let's begin by exploring the concept of unrealistic expectations, starting with the quest for "happiness." Many women have said they are not happy in their relationships. In many divorce filings, 'unhappiness' is cited as a key reason for ending a marriage. This raises an important question: if the romantic approach—characterized by grand engagements, lavish weddings, and passionate beginnings—is supposed to lead to a fulfilled life, why do so many people ultimately say, "I'm not happy"?

Let's take a closer look at a few case studies—starting with one from the American Sociological Association (ASA) in 2015, which revealed that nearly 70% of all divorces are initiated by women. This finding suggests that many women reach a breaking point in their marriages after repeated unmet needs and unaddressed concerns. When their efforts to improve the relationship go unheard, divorce often becomes their last resort—a necessary step to preserve their mental and emotional well-being. Because women tend to be more attuned to emotional disconnects and relationship issues, they're also more likely to take decisive action when things are no longer working, leading them to initiate divorce far more often than men.

Another study led by a Harvard-educated Ph.D. found that women initiate two-thirds of divorces in the U.S. The research, backed by a nationally representative study from the American Association of Retired Persons (AARP), analyzed the experiences of over 1,000 divorced men and women between the ages of 40 and 79.

The top reasons women gave for ending their marriages were verbal, emotional, and physical neglect. Interestingly, many of their husbands were utterly unaware of their wives' dissatisfaction. In fact, more than 25% of the men said they were blindsided by the news that their wives wanted a divorce.

Many of the men in the study shared that they believed they were supportive partners—but their focus was primarily on fulfilling their role as providers. These men felt intense pressure to maintain financial stability and continually raise their family's standard of living, often unaware that their wives were craving deeper emotional connection and support.

This study also reinforces a key point discussed in an earlier chapter—how men approach relationships differently. For many men, their primary focus lies in the household's economic well-being. They often compartmentalize their thoughts, treating each issue like a problem to be solved. So, when they're faced with a partner expressing unhappiness, they struggle—because emotional dissatisfaction isn't something that can be "fixed" with logic or material solutions.

This is where the disconnect becomes most apparent. When a woman says she's unhappy, it's not always about tangible needs—it's often about emotional connection, vulnerability, and affection. But many men, generally less expressive and less attuned to emotional nuance, fumble in these situations. Their partners' emotional needs go unmet, not out of malice, but from a lack of understanding or tools to respond.

So, when a divorce happens, men are left confused—thinking, *"But I bought the house, I put food on the table, I worked hard to provide—wasn't that enough?"* But for many women, while those things are appreciated, they're not the core of what makes a relationship fulfilling. Emotional intimacy, support, and feeling seen and heard often rank much higher on the list of priorities.

Some interesting parallels emerge if we compare this dynamic to the employee satisfaction index. Many employees report being dissatisfied with their jobs or careers, yet they don't quit. Why? Because the financial consequences of unemployment are too significant. Even if they're unfulfilled, they understand that losing a source of income could disrupt every area of their lives.

Now, apply that logic to relationships. If men could see the consequences of divorce—the emotional, financial, and familial fallout—they might be more proactive in addressing relationship issues before they reach a breaking point. But there's another side to this coin. Sometimes, a partner may shift expectations or move the goalpost, making it increasingly difficult for their spouse to meet their emotional needs. That dynamic can breed frustration on both sides.

It's also worth noting that divorce doesn't always lead to a happier ending. Studies show that many people who divorce don't necessarily find what they were missing in their previous relationship in the next one. This explains the pattern of multiple failed marriages or relationships—because the core issues often go unaddressed, only to resurface in new forms later on.

Staying in an unhappy relationship is not the solution. However, there are possible mediational steps that, when followed, can help in reconciliation. An amicable split could be the best outcome if that is not possible. The first step involves the couple discussing their fulfillment in the relationship and what it would take to be happy together. The second step is seeking professional intervention and help. This involves digging into how they got together in the first place. And here is the hard part: entering a relationship for reasons other than the purity of love, mutual attraction, and compassion will never work.

Many people cannot afford the cost of accountability, honesty, and truthfulness. This is because of the shame associated with the truth about why they are together, and this truth must remain in the shadows forever. Therefore, they find themselves in these relationships because of children, resources, security, and other factors. Thus, when lacking emotional fulfillment, a couple is more likely to get together for reasons other than love and attraction. Spoken or unspoken. Both men and women can struggle with transparency in their reasons for getting into a relationship. On the surface, both men and women might say and do what is expected of them without necessarily wanting to do those things out of love and attraction naturally. For women, they tend to give sex, and men offer protection and financial support. Since these three gestures imply deep care and affection, it is hard to determine why a couple can stay together. This truth is often bitter to swallow. So many people find themselves in prisons of love rather than the freedom of love.

Unlike jobs, relationships often have no immediate hardship consequences to encourage long-term commitment. So, it's not surprising that breakup and divorce rates are high. But it wasn't always this way. Traditionally, marriage was treated as an unbreakable covenant, not just a romantic bond. It involved two individuals and their extended families—and, in many cultures, even the larger community. When conflicts arose, in-laws or respected elders would step in to mediate and help find a resolution. Love played a role, but commitment to the covenant took precedence.

Fast forward to modern times, and the dynamic has shifted. Today, couples typically meet, fall in love, and decide to marry based primarily on personal feelings—often with little input beyond warm wishes from their families. As a result, when problems emerge, the decision to divorce is made solely between the two individuals, and the one who files often does so based on personal reasons that may or may not be fully disclosed. With fewer communal or structural ties reinforcing the relationship, it becomes easier to walk away when emotional needs aren't being met.

Suppose the romantic method was the only way of finding and securing a life partner. In that case, one might expect fewer breakups and divorces. However, as evidenced by recorded conflicts and breakups, this approach seems not to work. Examining what happiness means might help us in understanding this discrepancy.

In psychology, happiness is defined as a state of overall well-being and contentment. It involves experiencing primarily positive emotions, feeling satisfied with life, and having a sense of purpose. Understanding happiness in these terms challenges us to reconsider whether our ideas of romanticism might be setting us up for disappointment.

Psychologists often divide happiness into two main categories. *Hedonic* happiness is centered on seeking pleasure and avoiding pain, while *Eudaimonic* happiness is about living a meaningful life and realizing one's full potential. In short, happiness in psychology is about both feeling good and finding meaning. We can clearly see that in both cases, happiness is ultimately a personal journey, not something that is created solely within a relationship or from a partner.

When someone says they are unhappy in a relationship, they are genuinely expressing a lack of emotional fulfillment. In other words, they are ultimately dissatisfied with the relationship; it no longer serves its purpose (eudaimonic happiness), and they cannot find peace within themselves (hedonic happiness). This is a troubling realization because, in many cases, breakups and divorces are not just about incompatibility but one person's desire to live a fulfilled life. In cases where a partner has not done the work to find their actual psychological reasons for being unhappy, they can also project their internal dissatisfaction within themselves and life onto the relationship or their unsuspecting partner.

Essentially, the other partner gets hurt—not because they failed in their duties within the said relationship, but because they chose to be with someone who could not find happiness within themselves. In truth, the whole relationship can be a façade, whereby an emotionally deprived individual attempts to fill an empty life by feeding off another person's emotions under the false pretense of love.

This dynamic can be illustrated through a familiar analogy often seen in fantasy literature and film—vampires. These parasitic beings survive by secretly draining the life force from others. While dramatic, the metaphor speaks to a real and damaging relationship pattern: when one person depends solely on their partner for emotional fulfillment or happiness, especially at the partner's expense, they operate with a similar parasitic mindset.

It's like the story of a wealthy person constantly surrounded by fake friends. The moment the money runs out, those "friends" vanish. We've all heard stories of millionaires who went broke and were quickly abandoned. In the same way, when love becomes transactional—when someone stays only as long as their needs are being met—it stops being love and starts becoming exploitation. Real connections should be mutual, not one-sided.

A healthy relationship mutually requires two whole individuals to reciprocally choose to come together, not out of emotional deficiency, but from a genuine desire to connect, share, and experience life as a collective pair. The desire for partnership must voluntarily and intentionally arise from a place of strength ... not weakness.

The message here is clear: women and men must find happiness within themselves before entering a relationship. As previously discussed, many modern relationships struggle because one or both partners enter them emotionally unbalanced—seeking fulfillment *through* the other person rather than arriving with a sense of inner peace and wholeness to share.

When personal happiness depends on someone else, the relationship becomes fragile, overloaded with unrealistic expectations and pressure, making it difficult to sustain. Additionally, while romantic ideals still influence how we view love, there's a growing awareness today that emotional balance and self-awareness are critical to building a healthy, lasting partnership. Love thrives best when two whole people come together, not two halves looking to be completed.

A good relationship needs more than just strong feelings and deep chemistry. It also requires that both people get along well, share similar values, and make practical decisions together. When we see more divorces and breakups, it might be because some couples focus too much on romance and ignore these other important factors. Relying only on romantic love is not enough to keep a relationship strong over time.

While the appeal of strong emotional bonds remains, most men are now seeking and carefully evaluating their relationships by tactically making choices that will lead to long-term happiness and stability. In many cases, some men will unregrettably choose to remain single indefinitely.

So, the next time a friend confides that they're unhappy in a relationship, ask them *why*. More often than not, their dissatisfaction isn't just about arguments or routines—it stems from the expectation that the relationship should provide them with happiness and fulfillment. As they open up, you'll often hear deeper concerns: a lack of emotional connection, fading romance, or disappointment over what the relationship *was supposed* to offer.

One common oversight, especially among women, is entering long-term relationships without thoroughly evaluating their partner's emotional presence and stability. It's not that women should suppress their own emotional needs or expect men to "complete" them. Instead, women should seek emotionally available and compassionately invested partners—men who can nurture, support, and show up fully in the relationship. Emotional compatibility is not a luxury; it's a foundation. Without it, even the strongest chemistry can eventually feel hollow.

Additionally, not all women feel a heightened desire for emotionally available men. Some women are very comfortable with men who are less expressive emotionally. This is why a woman must know herself before engaging in a partnership where she knows there is a high chance her needs will not be met. It should be tiring and shameful to complain about partners who fail to meet our needs when we aren't equipped to pick the best partner to love in the first place.

Happiness in a relationship is not about what it gives us but what we bring to it. Emotionally unstable individuals will inevitably bring instability into their relationships. It's remarkable how avoidance of accountability plays a role in failed relationships.

For example, a woman with a serial dating mindset is more likely to fixate on her partner's flaws. Subconsciously, this may stem from a deeper fear: the realization that she herself may not be fully equipped for a lasting relationship. In response to this fear, she scrutinizes her partner, often searching for reasons to leave rather than stay. This mindset is often fueled by the belief that someone better is out there. But in reality, that belief is a gamble. Yes, there *might* be a better partner—but in many cases, there may not be.

Leaving a relationship that no longer serves its purpose can be a healthy and necessary decision. However, it should come with a clear understanding: there is a real possibility that a new, fulfilling partnership may not be easy—or even possible—to find. The current dating landscape doesn't exactly inspire confidence; fewer people are pursuing serious relationships or marriage, and the pool of emotionally available, committed partners seems to be shrinking. So, while walking away is sometimes the right choice, it's not without its risks—and should be approached with both courage and caution.

Ultimately, healthy relationships require self-awareness, accountability, and emotional stability. When someone struggles with commitment, jumps from one relationship to another, or avoids addressing challenges within a relationship, it often reflects emotional immaturity. The ability to stay, work through issues, and grow alongside a partner isn't just about love—it's a sign of maturity and a willingness to build a lasting relationship. Seeking emotional fulfillment from a partner is not the right approach to a healthy relationship. However, emotionally contributing to the relationship is the best approach. Suppose a woman experiences an emotional deficiency from her partner. In that case, she should inform and show her partner how she would want this need met. It is incredible how mature people expect their partners to be mindreaders. *A partner who is not emotionally available does not know how to be emotionally available.* Punishing a partner or breaking up with a partner who does not know how to fulfill her emotionally highlights a woman's poor choices in love. Because while he's emotionally unavailable, she chooses to date and enter a relationship with him. This sounds harsh, but for women to find happiness and fulfillment, they must also acknowledge that simply entering a relationship because a man is available does not work. Instead, seeing his values, emotional stability, and the capacity to sustain a relationship is important.

Sometimes, people who struggle with finding fulfillment in their relationship have the grass is greener on the other side, 'mindsets.' Therefore, actions like infidelity, adultery, or casual relationships come into play because they are trying to find emotional fulfillment from any available outside sources they feel is missing.

This thus demonstrates that when people follow strict romantic ideals, they may overlook the problems and issues in their relationship. Instead of recognizing these issues, they blame their partners without taking responsibility and fixing things. They continue in their relationships, being close-minded with their partners are rigid and uncompromising.

Overall, it is essential for women always to remember that the '3' things all men desire most in a relationship are (1) Physical intimacy (sex), (2) Feeling respected (ego-driven), and (3) A deeper sense of belonging.

A deeper sense of belonging means that men prefer a relationship where their partner is not overly or socially fluid or too inviting toward other men. A woman who frequently entertains male friends at a high level may unintentionally create tension in her relationship. Men are naturally territorial beings, and if a man feels that his partner is too accessible to other men, it can lead to discomfort, distrust, uncertainty, and insecurity, ultimately threatening the stability and permanency of the relationship.

In addition, a lack of sexual intimacy or a decline in physical desire in the bedroom is often interpreted by men as a sign that another male may be present in her life, thus fulfilling her sexual wants and needs. Many men perceive it this way, whether or not it is true. They may naturally deduce this from her lack of physical intimacy with him.

On the other hand, if a woman's lack of intimacy is being strategically or intentionally used as a mind game or test for the man, it often backfires and sabotages the relationship.

Expectedly, when a man senses and experiences the void of physical intimacy or sex, his natural and inherent response is to seek validation elsewhere, which can sometimes lead to seeking intimacy with a new love interest or another woman to whom he is attracted.

In summary, from the man's perspective, mind games can prove lethal in relationships. While some men may attempt to confront or control the situation and triumph over the said mind games, most will simply walk away and seek a partner who aligns with their expectations. Thus, choosing the 'paths of least resistance.' Men assess a relationship's long-term potential based on a woman's genuine desire for them. What if these sexual and intimate indicators are missing and prove nonexistent without cause? In that case, his logical mind will struggle to see a future together.

It's wise for a woman to be strategic in relationships—but strategy should never become a mind game. If she genuinely has no desire for the man, then sticking to a calculated plan can lead to the outcome she expects. However, if she wants him and is simply playing "hard to get," she risks losing him entirely. No matter the intention, games, and manipulation have no place in genuine love and attraction. Real connection thrives on authenticity, not tactics.

In many cases, this pattern of men and women using sex as a means of control plays out repeatedly, making it more and more the norm rather than the exception in modern dating. So, instead of solely blaming a partner's behavior, reflecting on how a couple ends up in these situations with certain types of incompatible and unlikely partners is essential.

It would be helpful for women to ask themselves important questions during courtship or before going on a date. Is he simply charming and persuasive? She can also question her feelings on whether she is focused on his romantic gestures and gifts and how he 'makes her feel.' Again, I cannot emphasize enough that when a woman wears her emotions on her sleeve, she becomes more susceptible to manipulation by men who see her as easy rather than principled. Hence, women shouldn't be too friendly to men. There are numerous cases where men emotionally hurt women during dating and or while in a relationship. This happens because when women are too friendly in social gatherings or parties, some men can interpret their overt affection as being socially fluid. As stated earlier, socially fluid women are not taken seriously for relationships and commitment by men who seek either marriages or long-term relationships.

Additionally, if not careful, a woman in a committed relationship can find herself compromised in an emotional connection with a man disguised as "just friends." What begins as a harmless conversation between two friends can slowly cross boundaries and shift into more personal territory for the woman. Over time, she thus begins to share intimate details about her life, frustrations, and unmet emotional needs with her 'male friend' instead of her partner. And before long, she's no longer just talking—but begins to *lean* on this male friend for advice on navigating her relationship or marriage. Eventually, a deeper emotional connection forms with the male friend, leading to physical intimacy.

A woman must, therefore, exercise discernment when maintaining close friendships with another man while in a committed relationship. A male friend can quickly become a source of emotional comfort and, unintentionally or not, begin to fulfill needs her partner is unaware that it is being outsourced to another man.

The danger here is subtle but very much real and irreversibly palpable. Women who engage in this behavior may not realize that, while seeking comfort elsewhere from a male friend or counterpart, they are ultimately and emotionally starving their partner. As a result of this, when their emotional intimacy and that emotional bond with their significant other weakens, deteriorates, or becomes nonexistent, the relationship often begins to unravel and come undone. What starts off as a simple text message can gradually escalate into daily check-ins, emotional dependency, and eventually a full-blown affair.

In the past, this kind of behavior could be possibly hidden more quickly or not considered threatening and disrespectful. Still, in today's world, men are far less tolerant. They are constantly bombarded with warning signs and cues, consuming advice from social media influencers, particularly women who coach them on how to recognize when their partner may be seeking physical or emotional intimacy elsewhere. Thus, the level of awareness and plethora of information that men have today is truly unprecedented, making a woman's deception harder to conceal and allowing the man to have the upper hand in handling the relationship's viability or futility.

In some cases, emotionally unfulfilled women are drawn to charming men who reflect their own buried desires. A man who knows how to connect emotionally with a woman often understands what women want, making it easier for him to enter that emotional void. However, these problems don't appear in a stable and fulfilling relationship; they surface when emotional needs are unmet by either one or both partners.

For example, consider a party or nightclub where everyone is out to have a good time. Again, is this truly the best place to seek a healthy, lasting relationship? The environment itself encourages fleeting connections rather than deep commitment.

Understanding where and why we seek relationships plays a critical role in the quality and longevity of those relationships.

From a romantic and fun-loving viewpoint, men usually don't go to clubs or social gatherings looking for a serious partner. Remember, we've already discussed that men customarily only go there to have fun. In these environments, a man might be inherently attracted to a woman solely because of her appearance, body shape, or outfit. Still, he isn't thinking about her deeper values. Most men socialize and compete to see who gets the "prettiest woman" or the "baddest woman" in social gatherings or clubs. This competition is predicated on their ego, and while the attention is on a woman, the truth is that men are actually much more focused on who will be deemed and crowned as the alpha male in the room.

Men seeking a serious relationship will avoid approaching women at parties and nightclubs. They prefer to learn about a woman's values first. These "hard-to-get" types are not likely to be found in places meant for fun, where one-night stands are customarily common. In terms of flirting, harmlessly flirting is perfectly fine, especially when you're young and enjoying meeting new people. The real question here is, where do you draw the line?

It begins with a woman asking herself if she's unhappy with the outcome of being associated with the party life. While having fun, going home, and staying focused on her life goals may be one thing, getting involved in messy romantic ventures that result in heartbreaks is a different story.

In the United States, romantic chronicles for many people start in middle and high school, where we first experience rejection, heartbreak, and the social pressures of dating. The desire to be popular and associate with the "cool" crowd often shapes a young woman's perception of relationships, and these ideas can follow her well into adulthood.

For example, a childhood crush that never materializes into a real relationship might leave her with feelings of inadequacy and longing, making her question whether she is good enough. Similarly, seeing a star athlete or a highly admired classmate receive endless attention from other girls can reinforce the idea that only popular, wealthy, or successful men are worth pursuing.

These early experiences shape her dating preferences, often leading her to seek socially validated partners rather than focusing on deeper compatibility.

You've likely met her before. When she talks about relationships, her exes or current partners are often defined by their *titles*, *wealth*, or *social status*—not by their character, integrity, or their good deeds. She's quick to mention their fame, occupation, net worth, or the material things they own but slow to describe their noble qualities as human beings.

This woman is often impressionistic, valuing surface-level achievements over depth. To her, relationships can become status symbols—proof of success or desirability—rather than authentic, soul-nourishing connections.

Ask her why she broke up with her ex; she may struggle to answer meaningfully. Instead, she'll likely focus on how "important" or "successful" he was without genuinely reflecting on the emotional dynamics of the relationship.

But here's the truth: this isn't always malicious. It often stems from a deeper emotional wound. It is possible that during her childhood, caregivers emphasized the importance of *marrying up* or seeking men with a higher social standing and wealth. To her, love is subconsciously tied to success, not emotional security.

In some heartbreaking cases, a woman who is taught this mindset is likely to endure toxic or even abusive relationships with men who simply have her material and social hierarchy boxes checked and nothing else. She's likely to trade emotional fulfillment for financial status, believing external validation is more valuable than inner peace.

Sometimes, a young woman's male crush might lead to early motherhood or teen pregnancy, which can drastically change her future trajectory. While other girls might just be having fun, she, on the other hand, as a young, new mom, could end up feeling very isolated and unable to concentrate in school, possibly causing her to drop out. Such experiences derived from her fleeting and pubescent decisions... can potentially and adversely affect her throughout her adult life.

In short, baseless 'romantic ideas and notions can have serious and life-altering consequences. Since these ideas are taught from a young age through media, school interactions, and familial ties, many women find themselves stuck in a cycle of trying to find a man who can fulfill their fantasies rather than security with a meaningful sense of belonging.

Romanticism celebrates the power of love and the emotional highs that come from deep, passionate connections. It portrays love as a force strong enough to overcome any obstacle and elevate the human experience. And while there's undeniable beauty in that ideal, romanticism often overlooks critical foundations of a lasting relationship—namely, a partner's core values and character.

In its own way, romanticism serves as a reminder—whether intentional or not—that deep feelings must be grounded in practical choices. When we rely solely on our heart's desires, we risk becoming disillusioned when reality fails to match our idealistic expectations. True love isn't just about butterflies and emotional intensity; it's about choosing wisely and building a connection that can weather both highs and lows.

Following our hearts doesn't mean our hearts or intuitions are infallible or foolproof. In truth, both are shaped by the environments we were raised in, the examples we saw growing up, and our personal experiences. Without reflection, we risk mistaking emotional intensity for compatibility.

Love is important, yes, absolutely—but so is wisdom. Healthy relationships require more than feelings; they require discernment, self-awareness, and the willingness to look beyond chemistry to character.

Psychologists also believe that early childhood experiences greatly influence who we are attracted to. This means how we experience love as adults can often repeat patterns from our youth, which may hold us back from personal growth and true fulfillment.

Chapter 3

The Impact of Fairy Tales on Dating and Relationships

Whether we want to admit it or not, the ideas and narratives found in fairy tales are often misguided attempts to present so-called universal truths about human life. Yet, like many concepts shaped by industrialization, societal conditioning, and consumer culture, these "truths" deserve to be questioned—and, as society evolves, redefined.

This is especially true when it comes to fairy tales centered around relationships. As human beliefs, diverse cultures, and moral frameworks continue to shift, the one-size-fits-all love stories of the past no longer reflect the complexity of modern relationships. When we look closer, we see that many popular fairy tales have already been reimagined—modified, retold, and adapted to reflect changing values and a deeper understanding of what love and partnership truly mean today.

Take the story of Cinderella, for example. It has changed significantly. As most people know it today, the Cinderella story has French roots, but the story itself is much older. It exists in many cultures around the world.

The most famous version is by Charles Perrault, a French author who published Cendrillon in 1697. This version introduced iconic elements like the glass slipper, pumpkin carriage, and the Fairy Godmother, which became staples in the modern retelling.

However, Cinderella-type tales go way back. A Chinese version (Ye Xian) from around 850 A.D. and a similar story from ancient Egypt involving a lost slipper and a royal marriage. So, the "Cinderella" theme has been around for some time. Hence, the argument is about who wrote the first version. We do know that the French version written by Perrault has been retold many times; hence, many people are familiar with his version. What is similar across this theme is romance and a rescue mission.

It's important to remember that the French version of Cinderella reflects a distinctly French cultural perspective on relationships. While influential, that perspective doesn't represent the entirety of the world's cultural heritage. Its widespread popularity, however, has unintentionally promoted French ideals of romance and love on a global scale—shaping how other cultures interpret and portray love in various ways.

In summary, Cinderella is a fairy tale about a kind and gentle young woman whom her cruel stepmother and stepsisters mistreat after her father's death. Forced to work as a servant in her home, she remains kind-hearted and hopeful despite her hardships.

One day, the king announces a royal ball so his son can find a bride. Cinderella wants to go but is forbidden by her stepmother, who ruins her dress and leaves her behind. When all seems lost, a magical Fairy Godmother transforms Cinderella's rags into a beautiful gown with glass slippers and a pumpkin into a carriage. The magic will only last until midnight.

At the ball, the prince is captivated by Cinderella, but she must flee as the clock strikes twelve, leaving behind one glass slipper. The prince searches the kingdom, trying the slipper on every maiden. When he finds Cinderella, the slipper fits perfectly, and they live happily ever after.

This story is captivating and engaging. On the one hand, you have a wealthy young lady who is being mistreated after her father's death; on the other, you have a prince who needs to marry. The French culture has given us new ways of looking at romance. We learn coined words and physical expressions like "French Kissing" because of that influence. While some debate when the Cinderella story first emerged—possibly even earlier—its popularity has genuinely endured for generations, making it one of the most widely told and listened-to tales. Cinderella offers insights into the cultural expectations placed on women of that time, particularly regarding dating, courtship, family expectations, and marriage.

The story gained even greater popularity thanks to the power and reach of film and media. Walt Disney's animated version in 1950 brought the tale to life for millions, and the CBS

Rodgers and Hammerstein production of Cinderella in 1957 drew one of the largest TV audiences of its time. Popular culture couldn't get enough of this magical tale, and soon, it was heavily capitalized and commercialized.

For instance, lipstick products and perfumes in decorative faux glass slippers emerged. The story had become more than a tale—it was now a well-oiled marketing machine and a massive driving force in the lives and minds of young girls and women … all over the world.

The Making of a Queen

Queen Elizabeth II's wedding can be viewed as a modern-day fairy tale—not because it was imaginary, but precisely because it was *real*. Her marriage to Prince Philip marked the first royal wedding to be widely broadcast and publicized, capturing the attention of the entire world. While the monarchy was never modeled after the Cinderella story, this iconic union embodied many elements that fairy tales romanticized: elegance, tradition, devotion, and grandeur. For millions of girls and women, it became a symbol of timeless love and regal romance, igniting imaginations and setting a new standard for what a "fairy tale wedding" could look like in real life.

Inspired by the true events surrounding Queen Elizabeth II's unexpected ascension to the throne, here is a fictionalized retelling of those events. While on her trip to Kenya, Africa, and after the passing of her Father, King George VI—the story you are about to read imagines the emotional landscape and inner experience of a young princess not destined initially ever to rule.

In this section, and with the use of creative narrative... we will imagine and lightly explore what it must have felt like for Queen Elizabeth II during her final moments of Princesshood—far from home and beneath the beautiful skies of Kenya, Africa...and far away from her palace ... where duty would abruptly call her... and history would forever shift.

As the sun set over the vast Kenyan wilderness, the golden hues of twilight spread softly across the horizon. The gentle sounds of nature filled the air—elephants quietly feeding by the watering hole, birds singing their evening melodies, and leaves rustling in the warm breeze. The atmosphere was peaceful, almost sacred as if the land held its breath in anticipation.

Princess Elizabeth leaned against the wooden railing of the Treetops Lodge, her gaze fixed on the endless landscape of acacia trees. The sounds around her were soothing yet unfamiliar, a reminder of how far she was from the structured world of Buckingham Palace. Here, she felt light and free, as though the responsibilities awaiting her back home had temporarily faded into the distance.

The Treetops Lodge was no ordinary place. Built into the branches of ancient trees, it lets guests watch wildlife from above like quiet observers of nature's hidden world. Earlier that day, Elizabeth had admired a family of elephants led by a matriarch with calm strength and grace.

That night, she went to bed, gently lulled to sleep by the sounds of the African wilderness. But as she dreamed, her world quietly changed.

Far away, at Sandringham House in England, her father, King George VI, took his final breath. The man who had guided her through life and steadied her as a child was gone. His passing was as quiet and absolute as the stillness of the Kenyan night.

Morning on the savannah burst with a blend of colors as if painted by God's own hand. But today felt different. Elizabeth didn't wake to the gentle light of dawn but to a firm knock on her door—the knock that would change everything.

She opened the door to see her private secretary, his face calm but his eyes carrying the weight of what he had to say. "Ma'am," he said softly, pausing as though the words were too heavy. "I'm afraid there's news."

She didn't need him to say more. Grief tightened her throat, but she forced it down as a queen must. She closed her eyes briefly, remembering her father's warm face and how he called her "Lilibet." But this was not the moment for memories. It was the moment to lead.

As the sun climbed over the Kenyan plains, she dressed no longer just Elizabeth—but the Queen. The weight of her new role was invisible, but she felt it in every breath. When she stepped outside, the morning breeze rustled the trees, and the watering hole reflected her calm, steady expression. She was ready.

Philip gently retook her hand, but it felt different, stronger, and more certain this time. "We'll go home," he said quietly.

She nodded, her eyes fixed on the horizon. The path ahead was wide and uncertain, but there was no turning back. Her reign had begun, not with royal ceremonies or fanfare, but with the quiet rhythm of nature and the heavy ache of loss. She had ascended the throne, not in a grand palace, but under the vast African skies.

As their plane lifted off from the red soil of Nairobi, Elizabeth had already changed. The young woman who had marveled at elephants the day before was gone. In her place was a queen—resolute, steady, and unshakable, like the matriarch she had admired leading her herd.

They said she went to bed a Princess and woke up a Queen. But it wasn't the trees that had elevated her—it was destiny. Patient and relentless, it had waited for the perfect moment to shape her future. Now, the world would know her not as Lilibet, not a Princess, a daughter, or a wife, but as Queen Elizabeth II.

Even as a princess, her grand wedding 1947 brought joy and excitement. For Great Britain, it showed strength and tradition during the country's recovery. Her coronation in 1953 added to the opulent and fairytale-like charm, with golden carriages, beautiful dresses, and sparkling crowns creating the image of a fairy-tale romance and the rise to power. At a time when people wanted something uplifting, the Royal Family gave them that dream. And that dream was Queen Elizabeth II.

While the *Cinderella* story is a beloved classic that embodies the "rags to riches" theme, it doesn't quite reflect the complexities of real life. Cinderella, at its core, is a beautiful young lady "not average" from a wealthy household, "not poor," and mistreated by the stepmother, "jealous" but rescued and her dignity restored through a princess.

In reality, royal marriages are rarely fairy tales. When a prince marries, it is typically to a woman of noble birth or high social standing—often another princess—not a beautiful girl from humble beginnings. But Cinderella wasn't just an ordinary girl. In truth, she was the rightful heiress to her father's estate. Her stepmother, however, sought to erase that identity, reducing her to the role of a servant in her own home. Rather than being an underdog who rose from obscurity, Cinderella was someone whose rightful place in society was stolen. Without the intervention of the Fairy Godmother, her future would have remained bleak, hidden beneath the lies and manipulation of those who sought to suppress her.

Historically, royal families have maintained this tradition to preserve lineage, alliances, and social expectations. On the rare occasion that someone outside of aristocracy is welcomed into a royal family, that person usually brings exceptional qualities, influence, or significance—especially if their royal partner is in line for the throne.

The French Cinderella narrative, however, tells a slightly different story. While the theme of social status remains central, it opens the door for misinterpretation. On the surface, it appears to celebrate a classic rags-to-riches journey. But beneath that romanticized veneer lies the truth: Cinderella was never just an ordinary "servant girl"—she was a young, beautiful woman from an influential family. The prince did not marry beneath his station or rescue a helpless damsel. Instead, he married a wealthy heiress, partially disguised by circumstance and misfortune.

This version reflects the surface-level ideals of romanticism, promoting the notion that love alone—divorced from wealth, power, or social standing—can rewrite one's fate. But in reality, the story falls short of that ideal. Cinderella's transformation isn't a break from her status; it's a return to it. So, while the tale is beautifully told, it leans more toward fantasy than historical truth.

When the *Cinderella* story gained popularity, it aligned closely with societal expectations placed on young women— particularly around marriage. During that period, the average age of marriage had already begun to rise. Yet, many young women still felt immense pressure to marry in their early twenties. Those who remained single beyond that age were often made to feel as though they were being "left behind."

Despite these growing societal shifts, the hope of early marriage remained strong. Popular culture and media reinforced that marriage and family life were the ultimate milestones for a woman's fulfillment. At 18, a person was legally considered an adult. By their early twenties, many women were expected to have already secured a husband and begun building a home and raising a family.

Stories like *Cinderella* tapped directly into those dreams— offering reassurance that love could still arrive swiftly and beautifully and change everything, even if life hadn't yet gone according to plan.

However, if we take a moment to examine the expectations placed on young men, a different narrative emerges. While women were conditioned to anticipate marriage by their early twenties, young men were often more focused on other pursuits—such as education, sports, and establishing careers. Marriage was no longer a pressing expectation for them. Instead, maturity for men was linked to financial stability and taking on responsibilities, with the promise of sex often serving as a motivating factor for marriage rather than societal and familial pressures.

This expectation imbalance created a cultural divide in how young men and women approached relationships and life goals. While women were encouraged to prioritize marriage early, men were given more time to establish themselves before settling down.

However, this came with strict conditions and consequences. If a man had sex and got a woman pregnant, he was often pressured into a 'shotgun wedding' – which was a forced marriage based on out-of-wedlock pregnancy.

Whereby the father of the woman was said to have pressured the man, through the unapologetic threat of violence, as he stood in the back of the church with his shotgun pointing to the groom, ensuring that the man that impregnated his daughter said, "I do" when the time came to do so The concept of a 'shogun wedding' was to ensure protection, provision, ownership of responsibility, and acknowledgment and legitimization of the unborn child. For the father, the marriage was thus an atonement of sorts in honor of the chastity of his daughter, which he believed was defiled in the taking or loss of her virginity before marriage and a 'proper courtship and wedding.' Irrespective of whether the expecting couple was ready to enter the marriage, the shotgun ensured the exchanging of vows took place.

While young women had been groomed most of their childhood and lives for marriage and motherhood, men, on the other hand, were laden with prerequisites and demanding expectations to accomplish if they wanted to marry. These undue pressures and conflicting messaging eventually began to lose their impact.

Additionally, the media significantly promoted this idea through romance comics, magazines, and movies targeting young audiences. However, the goal wasn't necessarily to help people find love—it was mainly for commercial gain. Over time, romanticism grew into a massive capitalistic industry, shaping how love and relationships were marketed to the public.

The aftermath of this movement has left deeper psychological challenges for women compared to men. While men often face pressure to achieve success, women continue to feel the expectation of getting married and starting a family. Despite the uncertainty of finding "Mr. Right," many women still cling to the fairy tale idea of meeting their prince. Unfortunately, this often leads them down a path of disappointment, symbolized by the common phrase "kissing many frogs" along the way.

To make matters worse, modern perspectives are challenging the "happily ever after" idea that the Cinderella story promotes. Real-life experiences prove that the journey to love and fulfillment is far more complex than fairy tales suggest, leaving many women stuck between fantasies and deniers of the harsher realities.

This is clearly reflected in young romance and love stories aimed at the younger generation. Titles like "My Prince Charming" were specifically designed to fuel the romantic ideal, focusing on the girl finding her perfect prince. This romanticism movement marks a shift from traditional values of marriage and relationships toward a more modern view centered on happiness and pleasure.

However, young men were not, and still are not, held to the same romantic standards. Instead, they face different pressures focused on providing, protecting, and building wealth for future generations. This responsibility is a heavy burden, made even more challenging by the added expectation of meeting the emotional needs of young women and making them feel happy and fulfilled. The result is a complex dynamic where both genders face unique but unequal pressures in pursuing love and success.

The idea of finding the right man as a "happy ending" was often built on unrealistic expectations. Encouraging a girl, barely out of her teens, to dream of this reality by 24 is nearly impossible.

Many women, influenced by fairy tales and sometimes parental neglect, make lifelong decisions without fully understanding the balance between reality and purpose when choosing a partner.

As more opportunities open up for women in the workforce and leadership positions, the belief that women need a "Prince Charming" to rescue them, as seen in the Cinderella story, is now being challenged. The original idea was that the woman had to come from humble beginnings and marry a wealthy man to live "happily ever after." But this no longer makes sense when women over 21 have careers and sometimes earn more than men.

This shift was further complicated in the 1970s by the sexual liberation movement, where abortion and birth control became more accessible, reducing the pressure to marry just because of pregnancy. Additionally, women's financial independence has weakened the idea that they must seek men of wealth or status to secure their future. Advances in medicine and longer life expectancies have also added new challenges. With more years to navigate relationships, the chances for conflicts and temptations have increased, making the idealized "happily ever after" even more challenging to sustain.

Modernism, when viewed through a historical lens, reveals how rising expectations for marriage based on love and romance often conflict with traditional ideas of stability and purpose. Traditionally, marriage is primarily centered around practical considerations, such as property, financial security, and the husband's role as the breadwinner and protector. Today, these traditional roles are under pressure to adapt to changing societal norms.

The concept of virginity before marriage and the traditional nuclear family—consisting of a father, mother, and children—is no longer seen as the only valid model of marriage and family. Instead, society now embraces diverse structures and unconventional arrangements, including blended families, single-parent households, and 'various' sexual partners' preferences. This has created a more complex and varied understanding of what marriage and family can be... and should be.

These changes place significant strain on modern marriages. In an era that values individuality, personal fulfillment, and sexual freedom, the challenge of maintaining lifetime fidelity and long-term commitment has become increasingly complex. Balancing these shifting expectations has made the idea of marriage and family more complicated than ever before.

Recently, the media has redefined classic fairy tales like Cinderella by introducing strong heroine characters, as seen in Disney's 2013 animated film Frozen. This musical fantasy follows the journey of two royal sisters in the kingdom of Arendelle. Elsa, the older sister, struggles to control her magical ice powers.

Previous fairy tales where a charming prince's intervention was central to the storyline, Frozen shifts the focus away from romantic rescue. The absence of a "Prince Charming" as the primary hero marks a significant departure from traditional narratives, reinforcing that a woman's journey need not be defined by romantic fulfillment.

In this movie, we see two royal sisters, Elsa and Anna, in the kingdom of Arendelle. Elsa has magical powers that allow her to create ice and snow. Still, she hides them for fear of hurting others, especially Anna.

Elsa becomes queen after their parents die, but her powers are accidentally revealed during her coronation. In panic, she flees to the mountains and creates a magical ice palace, plunging Arendelle into an eternal winter. Anna starts looking for her, teaming up with an ice seller named Kristoff, his loyal reindeer Sven, and a funny-talking snowman named Olaf.

Along the way, Anna believes that only "true love" can save the kingdom and herself, as her heart becomes accidentally frozen by Elsa. The film leads to a twist ending where Anna's act of true love is not romantic—but sacrificing herself for her sister. This breaks the curse, and Elsa realizes that love is the key to controlling her powers.

Ultimately, the sisters reconnect, the kingdom is saved, and Elsa learns to embrace her gifts instead of fearing them.

Unlike traditional fairy tales that center on a "damsel in distress" awaiting rescue by a prince, Frozen focuses on family bonds—in this case, the relationship between two sisters working together to restore their kingdom. The narrative deliberately avoids romantic dependence.

When compared to Snow White and the Seven Dwarfs (1937), the contrast is clear. Snow White portrays a heroine whose innocence and gentle nature are central to the plot. Still, her fate ultimately hinges on a prince's kiss. Her rescue reflects the older fairy tale model, where male intervention is necessary for a happy ending.

As societal views on relationships continue to evolve, the traditional fairy tale concept of "happily ever after" is also transforming. No longer is fulfillment solely defined by romantic love or the attainment of a partner—especially for women. This cultural shift highlights the importance of educating and empowering women, particularly those who have been shaped by older narratives rooted in romantic dependency and self-sacrifice.

Why is this shift so significant? Moving away from the romanticization of relationships and marriage allows women to fully embrace a new reality—one where equality in access to resources, opportunities, and personal fulfillment is the standard. In this evolving landscape, both women and men are encouraged to seek wholeness as individuals rather than viewing happiness as something that only comes through union with someone else. It moves from collective identity through partnership to self-defined purpose and autonomy—a narrative where love is a choice, not a requirement for a complete life.

Chapter 4

Emotions

This chapter will focus on how emotions shape women's feelings and experiences in the world around them, particularly in relationships.

Emotions are the feelings we experience in response to different situations in life. They influence our thoughts, actions, and interactions with others. Some emotions arise instantly—like fear when startled by a loud noise—while others develop gradually, such as love and trust in a close relationship. Emotions are a fundamental part of being human, helping us steer daily experiences and make sense of the world around us.

Recognizing emotions is crucial, as they significantly shape how women perceive relationships, steering through challenging situations and building meaningful connections. Emotions are a powerful guiding force in decision-making and communication in every sphere of life, whether friendships, romantic partnerships, or family dynamics.

Women can cultivate greater emotional intelligence by becoming more aware of how emotions influence behavior. This awareness helps deepen self-understanding while empowering the woman to respond more thoughtfully. In this case, intelligence helps guide feelings. So, instead of reacting based on how one feels, the reaction comes after thinking about consequences and outcomes.

Elements that form an Emotion

Scientifically, the exact formulation of an emotion is still debated, but what is undeniable is that emotions exist and play significant and vital roles in our daily lives. The easiest way to recognize an emotion is by first examining our thoughts.

Think about something that makes you happy—almost instantly, you may feel excitement or joy, and your body releases hormones responsible for that good feeling. Now, think about something that makes you sad—your body reacts differently, perhaps preparing for a fight-or-flight response. This automatic process highlights how closely emotions are linked to our thoughts.

In simple terms, our thoughts create feelings that manifest physically—whether as a sensation, a mood, or an overall state of being. This is what we define as an emotion. For women, it is imperative to recognize that thoughts will always generate positive or negative feelings. Understanding this connection helps us manage emotions effectively, make better decisions, and maintain emotional balance in relationships. As the old saying goes, "Thoughts are Things."

An emotion, therefore, has an element of physical **response and actualization**, which refers to the body's natural reactions to different states. These responses happen automatically, often before we even realize them. In simple terms, this means that we are not consciously controlling these reactions; they just occur as part of our experience.

Imagine standing in front of a large audience, ready to speak. The room falls silent, and you can feel the weight of a hundred eyes fixed on you. The air is still so quiet that you can hear a pin drop. Suddenly, your mouth goes dry, your palms grow clammy, and your heart pounds deafeningly loud in your chest. Your voice wavers slightly as you begin to speak, and you struggle to steady it. These are all involuntary physical reactions triggered by the anxiety of public speaking. You didn't choose to feel this way; your body simply responded to the situation, preparing you to face the moment.

Let's shift the scene to something more fitting for this book—love and relationships. Picture yourself on a first date with a man you've been excited to see. The setting is a perfect candlelit dinner, soft music playing in the background—but you've spent most of the evening nervously adjusting your posture, ensuring your hair falls just right, and even controlling your appetite so you don't appear too eager. The conversation has flowed, but now, as the date ends, uncertainty creeps in. He's been polite, even charming, yet something about his demeanor seems distant. You wonder if he's unimpressed or if this might be the last time you see him.

A thousand thoughts race through your mind as he drives you home and walks you to your doorstep. You want him—you know that much. He's handsome, he checks all your boxes, and in this moment, all you crave is for him to say something magical, something that reassures you he feels the same way. But he's behind you as you step onto the narrow-paved walkway, not beside you. Your mind spins with curiosity—Is he admiring me, or is he already preparing to say goodbye? The crisp night air brushes against your exposed back, sending a shiver down your spine.

Then, just as you reach the door, you feel the lightest touch on your shoulder. You turn, expecting words, but his lips find yours before you can say something. The soft, textured press of your lipstick melts into the warmth of his mouth. A rush of electricity shoots through your body, your heart pounds, and your knees weaken beneath you. You're lightheaded, dizzy, and wholly lost in the moment.

This—this overwhelming rush of sensation, the heat spreading through your body, your heart racing, the involuntary shudder in your breath—is an emotional, physical response. Like experiencing fear and nervous jitters before a speech, love, and attraction trigger automatic reactions, ones you don't generally control but simply experience; it's the body's integral response to deeper emotions, whether anxiety, excitement, passion or the intoxicating pull of romance.

When I say subconsciously, I mean these reactions happen without your conscious effort. You don't decide to make your mouth dry or your heart race—it just happens as part of your body's natural way of processing emotions. These physical responses are a way for your body to prepare you for what it perceives as a stressful or high-stakes situation. Recognizing this can help us manage emotions better, knowing that our bodies are simply reacting to our thoughts that created a feeling rather than something tangible. This awareness helps us control the moment and the situation rather than the situation controlling us.

Another key element of emotion is how we mentally process experiences—how the brain interprets and assigns meaning to our feelings. Our thoughts, past experiences, and perceptions shape our emotional reactions in this stage.

For example, if we feel nervous before an exam, our brain links that feeling to the pressure of performing well. In relationships, we may experience anxiety or uncertainty if we interpret our partner's actions or words as signs of conflict. These emotional responses are deeply influenced by our core values and beliefs, which are primarily shaped during childhood and past relationships.

A minor miscommunication, a temporary lack of affection, or a moment without reassurance can feel overwhelming, sometimes leading to unnecessary distress or even a breakup.

Because our thoughts and interpretations play a significant role in how we respond emotionally, learning to control our thoughts is essential. By managing our perceptions and avoiding exaggerated reactions, we can prevent emotional meltdowns and misunderstandings, ensuring that simple disagreements don't escalate into major issues.

Imagine you've been dating someone for a while. You care about him deeply, but over time, you begin to wonder: *"Does he want to marry me?"* He works long hours—sometimes so much that you barely get quality time together. You want to call him a workaholic, but you hesitate, fearing how he might respond.

You equate his dedication to work with emotional avoidance as the distance grows. Then the doubts start creeping in, often fueled by conversations with your closest friends: *"He's not serious,"* they tell you. *"You should leave him for someone who's ready to commit."*

But let's pause and analyze that phrase: *"He's not serious."* What does that really mean? Does it mean he doesn't want the relationship—or that he's not giving you what you *expect* from the relationship right now?

This is where many women experience resistance from men. To a woman, *being serious* often means progressing toward marriage. However, marriage or long-term commitment is viewed very differently by men.

Men are typically only comfortable moving forward when they feel all the necessary elements for a successful relationship are in place. That includes financial stability, a suitable living situation, and emotional readiness. For men, commitment is less about timing and more about preparedness.

A woman may feel that *love is enough*—they can marry and figure out the rest along the way. But men tend to think: *Let me get everything together first, then we'll move forward.* They prioritize logic over emotion in this area, especially in today's world, where the pressure of being a provider weighs heavily. For many men, this responsibility cannot be transferred to their future wife—it's something they carry with pride and pressure.

So, when a man seems hesitant, it doesn't always mean he isn't serious in the relationship. It may mean he's gathering his essentials and building the foundation before taking the next step.

The worst thing a woman can do in that relationship phase is to seek advice from friends or family who may not have the complete picture or are navigating the same storm. Too often, single women take advice from other single women, creating a cycle of misinformed perspectives. As someone once said, *"How can someone who's in the same boat help you get out of it when they're still looking for the shore, too?"* It becomes a case of the blind leading the blind.

Back to the story

The woman begins to feel the pressure from every direction. Her friends and family aren't making things easier. They constantly remind her of the other men who've shown interest—men she's dismissed but who, according to them, might be more "serious."

"You haven't even mentioned that you're in a relationship," one friend points out. "He's probably taking your silence as permission to keep you on hold."

Even her mother joins in with concern masked as love: *"He's wasting your time,"* she warns. *"Your biological clock is ticking. You deserve someone serious about your future."*

The pressure builds quietly but consistently like water filling a glass. And in her mind, she's already had the conversation a dozen times—imagining what she'd say, how he'd respond, and how it might all fall apart.

Then, one weekend, he takes her to a beautiful restaurant. The ambiance is perfect: soft lighting, gentle music, and a table tucked away just for the two of them. But despite the setting, she can't relax. Anxiety gnaws at her, louder than the music, heavier than the meal.

As dessert arrives, she can't hold it in any longer. She puts down her fork, looks him in the eye, and asks:

"What are your future plans for us?"

He looks up, momentarily caught off guard. There's a flicker of surprise in his eyes, which frustrates her. *Why doesn't he see this coming? Why doesn't he already know what she needs to hear?*

She pushes further.

"Do you see us getting married in the future?"

He pauses, then replies with a calm but disarming question:

"Why do you ask?"

The response stings. It feels like a dodge. Her frustration boils.

She takes a breath, trying to stay composed but unable to hide her disappointment.

"Because I've been thinking a lot about us. About how things are going. And honestly? I'm starting to believe you're not interested in a serious relationship... one that leads to marriage."

His expression hardens, and his jaw clenches—the mood shifts.

"Where did you get that idea from?" he snaps, his tone sharper than she expected.

And just like that, the conversation becomes more than just about the future—it becomes about misunderstanding, unmet needs, and two people sitting at the same table but feeling miles apart.

A wave of anxiety rises in her chest, and without thinking, she blurts out, "Even my friends and my mother think you're not serious about us."

The words hang heavy in the air. Silence follows.

He leans forward, his expression unreadable at first then softens as he meets her eyes. His voice, quiet and tender, breaks the stillness.

"I'm sorry you feel that way," he says. "There is no one I love more than you. I only wish your friends and mother had more faith in me—in *us*, babe."

She opens her mouth to respond, ready to defend her friends and mother, but the waiter arrives just in time—carrying a silver-covered platter. Dessert, it seems.

As the lid lifts, her breath catches. Sitting on the plate is a dazzling diamond engagement ring designed and specially customized for her. It must have taken months for him to plan such a beautiful surprise, this dinner, the engagement. She messed everything up because of assumptions, impatience, negative influence, and commentary from her family and friends. For a moment, she freezes. Her thoughts race. Did he hear everything she just said and admitted? Has she ruined the moment with her doubts? What will her friends and mother say now?

A surge of emotions floods her—shock, shame, guilt, joy, and an overwhelming wave of love. Her vision blurs as tears fill her eyes. Looking up, she sees him kneeling before her, holding the ring in both hands, his gaze steadily filled with transparent vulnerability and hope.

Her heart pounds in her chest, so loud she's sure it can be heard by the other guests dining across the restaurant. Her breathing becomes shallow and hastens as the butterflies overtake her stomach. All the while, the tears in her eyes threaten to spill over and cascade down her face. Shamefully, all her previous thoughts, feelings, and instincts about her relationship's status and lack of progress collide in a storm and conundrum of realization, shock, and self-humiliation.

This is the moment every little girl dreams of. The lights, the anticipation—and then, just as her heart swells, he utters the most unexpected and painful words.

"Baby," he says softly, "I don't think you're ready. I love you deeply and want to ensure your family and friends feel at peace with this. But I feel humiliated now, knowing your mother has no faith in me." He pauses, his voice thick with emotion. "Today was supposed to be our moment. I've been planning it for months... dreaming of this very night. But now, I'm not sure the feeling is mutual."

Still, he looks up at her on one knee, his eyes full of love and hurt. "I memorized the words I wanted to say when asking you to marry me. You're the love of my life. But tonight, you can take this ring instead of a proposal. Show your mom. Show your friends. Let them know that I wanted to propose tonight formally."

"I'm not asking you tonight. Let me know when I'm welcomed into your family. Hopefully, you'll wear this ring the next time I see you."

With that, he leans in, still on one knee, kisses her hand tenderly, gets up, and leaves after paying plus tip. He does not look back.

This is the moment where emotional presence matters. Her response, whether marked by hesitation, joy, or regret—will shape the direction of everything that comes next and will shape the rest of her life with or without him.

You see, it's no longer just about the ring or about the actual proposal. It's about trust, timing, and whether she lets 'love' … rise above her unfounded fears.

This is why emotions are essential, but even more importantly, learning to control and understand them is the key to success in relationships. As a woman, mastering emotional intelligence can make the difference between strengthening a relationship or unknowingly destroying one, resulting in the pushing away of someone you are highly compatible with. Taming emotions doesn't mean ignoring them; it just means understanding them and allowing them to guide you wisely rather than recklessly. Because in love, just like in life, emotions can either build a bridge or burn one down. The choice will always be yours.

The last aspect of an emotion is the outward expression of it, which is how we display emotions through body language and facial expressions—such as smiling when joyful, shedding tears when sad, or folding arms when frustrated.

Emotions don't just stay inside of us; they manifest in the ways we speak, move, and react to our partner's words and actions. Love particularly has a way of making itself known through outward expressions, whether it's through tender touches, longing glances, or even unspoken gestures. These physical and verbal cues communicate what words sometimes cannot, thus revealing our deepest and innermost feelings.

Take this moment, for example. Imagine you're in love with someone, and tonight, you both meet after weeks of being apart. The anticipation has been building, and even though you've been texting and calling, nothing compares to being in each other's presence. As soon as you see him, your body reacts before your mind even catches up—your breath quickens, your face lights up with an uncontrollable smile, and you rush toward him for a huge reunifying embrace without thinking.

He barely has time to open his arms before you leap into them while wrapping yourself around him, squeezing him tighter than you intended. Your fingers instinctively clutch his jacket as you try to visually devour him and take in his mere presence as quickly as possible, as if afraid he'll disappear again. When he laughs in response to your unapologetic vulnerability, tremendous affection, and emotional candor in your happiness in seeing him, his laugh sounds even better than you remembered. It's warm, familiar, masculine, and infectious. Oh, how you missed him, so you pull back ever so slightly, only to be able to successfully cup his face in your hands while studying him and memorizing him. Your eyes shimmer with excitement and glisten with tears, and though you don't mean to, they betray you, revealing just how much you've missed him and have longed for him. This is love in all its genuine, candid, and expressive glory.

He sees it. He feels it. Some things cannot be feigned or forch when genuinely expressed through unconditional love. Instead of speaking, he simply presses his forehead against yours, his hands resting at your waist, his breath mingling with yours. The world fades; no one else matters at that moment, and no words are needed. Your outward expressions—your tender embrace, your seductive and loving gaze, your trembling fingers slowly tracing his jawline—say everything. Love

Understanding Emotional Maps

An *emotional map* can be considered an internal guide. This personal framework influences how we process feelings, handle relationships, and respond to conflict. This map isn't something we're handed at birth; it forms gradually, shaped by our surroundings, experiences, and the people who raised us and to whom we were exposed to at a young age.

No one enters the world in perfect condition, and our caregivers—parents, relatives, or legal guardians—carry their own emotional histories, frameworks, and backstories. These histories often become the lens through which we learn how to socialize and connect.

In our earliest days, as infants, we begin exploring the world through our '5' senses. This stage, often called *sensory discovery*, becomes the groundwork of emotional learning. We first recognize our caregivers not by logic or language but by the comfort of their touch, the familiarity of their scent, and the calming rhythm of their voice or heartbeat when lying on their chest. Long before our eyes can see, our bodies are already learning what safety, connection, and attention feel like.

These early impressions leave a lasting imprint. Hence, a caregiver's unique and distinctive influence on an impressionable child proves invaluable. They quietly teach us how to respond to closeness, trust, and protection. Over time, these moments come together to form the emotional framework we carry into adulthood—often without realizing it.

We find comfort in familiar sounds, such as our mother's heartbeat or the rhythm of her voice, which provides a sense of security.

The next stage is Emotional Bonding, where the sensation of being held, fed, and comforted builds our early emotional connections, teaching us that we are safe and cared for. As we grow older, our emotions form based on our interactions with our caregivers. We develop a sense of trust if our needs are met with warmth and consistency. Our caregiver's smiles, soothing words, and gentle touch reinforce feelings of love and security.

However, suppose they are inconsistent in their care or neglect our needs. In that case, this creates uncertainty, making us anxious or hesitant in future interactions. The next stage is Curiosity and Learning. During this stage, we display high levels of natural curiosity. We discover movements as we gain control over our bodies, especially limbs. As children, we begin to reach for objects, explore our surroundings, and react to new things and objects. We get excited about every experience—whether it is a touch from our caregivers or the taste of food (hopefully, our caregivers are present because, as children, we will put anything in their mouths), we are delighted by the feeling of a variety of textured objects and multiple colors, and new sounds easily amuse us. At this stage, our little brains form consistent patterns and thoughts while assigning an emotion to every experience. Cognitively, we begin to pair up, cause and effect.

During the toddler stages, we begin developing *social awareness*—the ability to recognize and respond to the emotions of others. This is when children start to mirror facial expressions, imitate behavior, and respond to varying tones of voice. Even without fully understanding words, a toddler can sense whether a caregiver is joyful, angry, or stressed by listening to voice inflections and observing body language.

For example, a raised or sharp tone can signal tension, while a gentle, playful tone brings comfort. This sensitivity is part of how toddlers interpret the world around them.

It's important to understand that when young children are exposed to conflict—particularly verbal disagreements between parents or caregivers—it can create feelings of insecurity. A child's need for emotional safety and consistency is critical at this early developmental stage. When the home environment becomes unpredictable or emotionally volatile, it disrupts the child's sense of stability and belonging.

This is the reason why parents and caregivers must be mindful of their actions, words, sporadic or toxic outbursts, and emotional energy. Children are not passive observers—they absorb the emotional atmosphere of their environment. What they witness in their early years significantly shapes how they relate to themselves and others later in life.

Children are incredibly perceptive, highly impressionable, and quickly learn to pick up on verbal, non-verbal, and social cues. Even when young, they mimic words and behaviors they observe in their caregivers. For instance, if a caregiver firmly says "No," a child may repeat the phrase, imitating the tone and intensity. Simple gestures like laughter, hugs, and consistent eye contact begin to teach children what affection and emotional connection feels like. Conversely, being ignored, scolded, or met with frustration also shapes their understanding of social expectations and boundaries.

As children grow, they enter a crucial stage known as the *development of independence.* During this stage of their development, their perspective begins to shift—shaped by experiences from infancy through the toddler years. They naturally start to crave autonomy, not dependency. They test boundaries, challenge authority, and frequently question the rules set by caregivers.

The classic question "Why?" becomes their way of asserting curiosity and critical thinking. They no longer accept "No" at face value and begin to express their preferences, wants, and emotional responses more clearly—whether joyful or defiant.

This stage also introduces a heightened awareness of their environment. Home becomes familiar, and they start to crave novelty and exploration. A simple trip to the park, a new playground, or a walk in nature can bring tremendous excitement as the child seeks new experiences that stimulate learning and growth.

Ultimately, this period lays the groundwork for identity development. Children begin to understand how to explore the world and how they fit within it—emotionally, socially, and physically.

An *emotional map* functions much like our memory. Just as the brain stores information about places we've visited, people we've met, and activities we enjoy, it also stores the *feelings* attached to those experiences. Emotions, in this way, act as labels on our memories—marking each one with a sense of meaning.

For example, many people can vividly recall moments from a favorite childhood holiday—unwrapping gifts, playing with new toys, and laughing with family. The joy felt in those moments becomes an emotional stamp on the memory. That sense of *happiness* gets encoded along with the sights, sounds, and smells. The entire experience becomes a cherished part of our mental landscape.

This process works the same with painful and traumatic experiences. When a child experiences trauma—whether through emotional neglect, physical harm, or mental abuse—the brain attaches *negative emotions* to those events. The memory is stored, but with feelings like fear, sadness, or shame attached. Later in life, when something similar happens—an argument, rejection, or even a specific tone of voice—the brain retrieves that emotional memory, and the same painful feelings can resurface.

This is the essence of an emotional map: our ability to trace a current emotional reaction back to an earlier experience. It helps to explain why we sometimes feel deep sadness, anxiety, or even unexplained joy in situations that echo our past.

Understanding emotional maps allows us to uncover the hidden roots of our emotional responses in adulthood. Identifying where certain feelings originate, we can begin the healing process, break unhealthy patterns, and respond to life with greater awareness and emotional clarity.

How Emotional Maps Impact Relationships

We can, therefore, now conclude that emotional patterns formed during childhood deeply influence how we experience love, intimacy, and self-worth in adulthood. Family dynamics, parental relationships, and societal expectations shape emotional maps. When emotional needs go unmet during childhood, they leave lasting imprints that affect how we steer romantic relationships.

For both men and women, childhood experiences—whether it's emotional neglect, inconsistent affection, or witnessing unhealthy relationship dynamics in their parents or caregivers, set the foundation for their future relationships.

A woman who grew up feeling unseen or unheard may struggle with low self-worth, leading to patterns of seeking validation from romantic partners. Additionally, she may experience heightened anxiety whenever she perceives rejection. Women who were told they were beautiful growing up are likely to think that others are jealous of their looks, even when commentary on beauty is unwarranted since all women are uniquely beautiful in their own ways. Others who witnessed their mothers endure toxic relationships may unconsciously repeat similar cycles, believing that love must come with struggle or sacrifice. These emotional blueprints influence their choices, from the partners they select to how they communicate, handle conflict, and define their self-worth in relationships.

Psychologists suggest that women are often drawn to partners who reflect familiar emotional patterns from their past—even when those patterns were unhealthy. This unconscious attraction explains why many women find themselves stuck in repetitive relationship cycles: choosing emotionally unavailable partners, feeling chronically unfulfilled despite being in a relationship, or struggling with trust and attachment issues.

The subconscious mind has a way of seeking resolution. It attempts to *complete* what was left unfinished in childhood— reaching for the love, security, or affirmation that may have been lacking early in life. As a result, some women are unknowingly drawn to partners who resemble the emotional environment they once knew, even if it was toxic or emotionally damaging.

Rather than healing the wound, these relationships often reopen it. What starts as an opportunity for love becomes a mirror non-discriminatorily reflecting past unresolved pain and trauma. Until those early experiences are acknowledged and processed, the cycle tends to repeat, creating disappointment, confusion, and emotional exhaustion.

This explains why deep romantic attachments can feel overwhelmingly intense for some women. Love is often described as fulfillment, with phrases like "He completes me" or "I feel whole with him." These emotions stem from an unconscious desire to fill the emotional voids left by childhood experiences. It is vital to clarify that this void is healthy and not unhealthy. Feeling whole or complete in a relationship equates to emotional fulfillment.

Hence the reason, many women, especially in the early stages of love, display childlike behaviors—seeking comfort, reassurance, and emotional security from their partners— because their unconscious mind associates romantic intimacy with the nurturing they may or may not have received as children. However, when childhood wounds remain unresolved in an individual, relationships can become emotionally exhausting.

The fear of rejection, abandonment, or being "insufficient" can create deep insecurities, leading to unhealthy attachments. Unlike learning a skill such as cooking or speaking a new language, love, and relationships are deeply tied to emotional patterns or maps, making them that much harder to change.

For instance, when a woman experiences rejection in dating, it may not be about that moment, the men she meets, or how those dates went. Instead, her unconscious mind may be reliving every instance of feeling rejected during her childhood and the pain, shame, and internal turmoil it caused her — whether it was feeling unloved by a parent, being dismissed by authority figures, or struggling to receive emotional validation.

This is why being "ghosted" or "stood up" on a date can feel particularly disproportionate and very painful for her because it triggers deep-seated fears of abandonment and rejection that have been ingrained and embedded into her psyche since childhood.

Thus, breaking free from unhealthy relationship patterns requires *self-awareness* and *intentional healing*. The good news is that emotional maps are thankfully not permanent—and can be healed, revised, reshaped, and reconfigured. The first step in this process is *self-reflection*—an honest evaluation of past experiences, especially the memories that continue to trigger emotional reactions, and how women can learn to cope with how to prevent such triggers from forming.

Unfortunately, for many women, breakups don't always bring closure. Lingering emotions and unresolved feelings about a former partner often remain simmering and dormant beneath the surface. When these emotional ties aren't correctly or even professionally addressed and properly severed, they can easily resurface in future relationships, disrupting what could've been an amazing fresh start with the right man.

It's not uncommon for women to seek comfort in old flings or familiar relationships after a breakup. What begins as a temporary refuge can turn into a dangerous and unfulfilling habit where past lovers will remain in the "friend zone." At the same time, new relationships with other men are being pursued on the side by the women in the interim. Over time, this behavior can develop into a serial dating pattern driven by the pursuit of a perfect connection that never materializes.

A woman who keeps ex-lovers close without fully resolving those emotional attachments has not truly mastered the art of maturely moving on. Often, breakups such as these...weren't rooted in dire and toxic situations involving some form of abuse, betrayal, or profound incompatibility. Instead, they are rooted in the woman's temporary and momentary dissatisfaction, feeling that her expectations are sometimes unjustifiably unmet, or her anxiety over an existing emotional discomfort. Sadly, when some women sense a challenge in their relationship, they may hastily break things off too quickly to regain a sense of subjective control or peace in life—but in hurriedly doing so, they avoid *complete detachment*. The ensuing toxic remnants of unresolved emotional detachments with her partner will remain indefinitely.

These unresolved cycles prevent true healing for the woman. Without the ample space and time needed to reflect and release the past, her emotional map remains unchanged, making engaging in a new relationship difficult. Therefore, her new relationship exists in the shadows of old ones. Absolute freedom comes when a woman cuts *ties entirely* with what no longer serves her growth and intentionally creates space for a new, healthier version of love.

Many men are unaware that, often, when a woman begins to distance herself emotionally—and especially just before or shortly after a breakup—there's a high likelihood that she has reconnected with someone familiar, such as an old flame or old lover from her past. This behavior is driven by more than the old saying, *"The devil you know is better than the devil you don't."*

It's similarly and unavoidably rooted in her *emotional map*—and causes a subconscious pull toward the past where there may have been a sliver of comfort, connection, passion, a safety blanket, or a hint of unresolved hope. Suppose she ended that previous relationship prematurely or without the necessary closure. In that case, she may return to that relationship not just out of loneliness but to see if there is a possibility of salvaging what remains. This is done under the notion and optimism at times of the delusional idea of what if.

True healing and forward movement, however, require intentional self-inquiry. For a woman to grow, she must pause and examine her thoughts before taking action. Suppose her current partner isn't meeting her emotional needs; instead of running back to the past or abruptly ending the relationship, she can also ask herself essential questions like, *Why do I withdraw or leave every time whenever I'm faced with a challenge? What am I truly seeking?*

Developing stronger internal beliefs—grounded in self-worth, patience, and emotional resilience—creates a more centered and stable life. Those with the mindset that *"there's always something better out there"* often find themselves in a cycle—making loops through relationships, only to circle back to square one. Whereby it is at square one that the woman will begin to realize that regardless of the 'something better out there,' without putting in the work or taking accountabilities for her life's actions and choices, attempts to land a fulfilling relationship ... will prove futile. Breaking the cycle starts with looking inward, not by looking backward.

Many men have shared that their ex-partners, who ended the relationship in their pursuit of a long-term commitment or marriage with other men, often still found themselves single—

or are still searching for that proverbial 'perfect man'—years after the breakup.

This isn't to say that the breakup with the ex-partner was never justified. Still, it highlights an important truth: that walking away doesn't automatically mean a better partner is waiting on the other side, who, against all odds, will guarantee a seamless relationship or guaranteed happiness. Relationships take work. Self-work. Internal work. Mutually reciprocal and intentional work

Sometimes, the real solution lies not in leaving but in becoming accountable for *how we show up* in a relationship. Without doing the inner work, we risk repeating the same cycles—chasing ideal outcomes without changing the mindset or behaviors that prevent meaningful connections. Eventually, the pattern becomes obvious. After several failed relationships, the common denominator is no longer them—it's *us*.

When someone continually blames their partners for every breakup, it becomes increasingly complex to ignore the truth: unresolved issues within *ourselves* may be the root cause. Without self-reflection and healing, we risk becoming the person we claimed we were trying to avoid. In other words, the 'victim' in the past relationship becomes the 'perpetrator' or 'bully' in the new one.

Open communication plays a vital role in this process. Clearly expressing needs, setting healthy boundaries, and listening with empathy contribute to more sustainable, fulfilling relationships.

Whether through personal growth, counseling, or inner work, healing past wounds thus empowers women to stop seeking validation from others and instead build a stronger, more grounded sense of self-worth. When we grow from within, we stop trying to fix people—and start attracting partners who are aligned with the healed, whole version of ourselves.

Why We Are Drawn to Certain People

Attraction isn't solely based on physical appearance—it's deeply rooted in an *emotional familiarity* that sometimes cannot be explained. Our emotional maps, shaped by our early childhood experiences and evolving relationship experiences, quietly influence whom we are drawn to, often without our conscious awareness.

When someone's energy, behavior, or personality reminds us of a nurturing parent or a first love, we may feel an instant connection. On the other hand, if someone invokes our unresolved emotional wound, we may still gravitate toward them—subconsciously seeking to rewrite the past or obtain the closure we never received.

Making this even more complicated and complex is that our subconscious doesn't tap us on the shoulder and say, "You're *chasing the past again."* Instead, it disguises the familiarity as something new, promising, and hopeful.

Only through reflection—and examining our patterns and past relationships—do we realize that many of our partners share a common thread. Sometimes, the thread can be external—like the importance of a man's appearance. Physical attraction plays a significant role for many women, especially when it comes to a man's body type or height. But beneath all that, there's another unspoken layer and the delicate topic many women may want to avoid or coat over: a woman's age and its impact on her dating, relationship possibilities, and a man's desirability towards her.

Overall, a woman's age can be deemed both an asset and, in many ways, a limiting factor—especially as it relates to how much time she needs to find "the one successfully." In her younger years, she may have had the flexibility to peruse and explore, take risks, and freely walk away from relationships that didn't serve her needs or align with her desires. Unfortunately for her, the dating landscape and paradigm completely shift as she matures. It is not necessarily because there are fewer available men out there but because *fewer men are actively seeking women within her age* bracket.

Here's how it works: A man of the same age may be at a point in life where he's either ready to settle down and start a family— or he's already chosen to remain single and avoids long-term commitments altogether. So, suppose he meets a woman his age who is single as well. In that case, he may not view her as a potential option because of the existing mismatch, and one wants a long-term relationship while the other is seeking a friend with benefits. This is not because she lacks value but because his mindset about family, timing, biological clocks, and emotional investment has already shifted.

This isn't to say that meaningful love can't happen later in life—it absolutely can. Yet, the habit of repeatedly breaking up and starting over—especially without doing the necessary healing work—can be just as counterproductive as launching a new business every time your existing business experiences challenges in growth. Those challenges will strengthen both the business and the owner. Quitting is not always a solution in most cases. At some point, *time* becomes the deciding factor, not just opportunity and access to available prospects in the dating market.

Women must thus begin to view *time* with greater value and seriousness. After age 30, the dating pool doesn't vanish but becomes more complex. This is why healing and emotional self-work are essential—not just to maintain relationships but to avoid unnecessary breakups rooted in unresolved issues. There comes a time when our reasons for being alone no longer make sense—not to others or ourselves.

Ultimately, time remains our friend—*but only if we recognize its value and use it wisely.*

A person who grew up feeling emotionally neglected might be drawn to emotionally unavailable partners, trying to "win" their love to heal their past wounds. While someone raised in a secure, affectionate environment might naturally seek a relationship that mirrors that warmth and stability. Here is where one size doesn't fit all.

Emotional Triggers: When the Past Resurfaces

You must know that our emotional maps all contain markers—or points where we've experienced love, loss, betrayal, or joy. When a new partner does something that reminds us of a past wound, we react to the present moment and the history behind it. This is why minor disagreements can unjustifiably escalate: they are secretly or unknowingly often connected to something much deeper than the current contentions at hand.

Let's apply the above concept. If a past partner was dismissive during arguments, even a simple *"let's talk later"* from a new partner can trigger intense feelings of abandonment and past condescending wounds, unrelatable and unassignable to the new partner. Yet a partner who struggles with abandonment can be easily triggered to apply the past wounds to the new relationship.

Similarly, if someone with unresolved abandonment issues hears phrases like *"I need some space"*—whether it's needed for processing a situation or dealing with work stress—it often stirs a more profound anxiety in the partner that suffered past instances of abandonment. What feels like a normal boundary to one person can feel like emotional rejection to another.

When past or current issues of abandonment haven't been rightfully or professionally addressed, those being affected by internal episodes and struggles may wrongfully handle the matter by abruptly and indefensibly ending the relationship with the guiltless and unsuspecting new partner prematurely. Why, you ask? It is because it feels somewhat selfishly safer to reject someone else before opening yourself up to the 'possibility' of being the one to be rejected or dismissed.

In essence, this person thus succeeds in preemptively sabotaging relationships and attempting to prevent this unseen 'possibility' of heartbreak, ironically creating heartbreaks themselves. This causes personal fears and internal turmoil within, positioning them in a constant state of hyper-vigilance, where every word, delay, or change in tone is analyzed under an unconscionable and undeserving microscope.

This emotional pattern usually begins in childhood. Perhaps a sibling needed alone time, and it was misinterpreted as rejection. Without a parent or caregiver to gently explain that *needing space is normal*, the child internalizes that being left alone means being unloved.

Over time, this belief becomes embedded in the child's emotional map as they evolve into adulthood. And as they mature and enter romantic relationships, those early wounds don't disappear—they evolve. They surface in subtle yet destructive ways, often unraveling relationships with people who could offer healing.

This unresolved pain can also explain why some women keep their ex-boyfriends in the friend zone after a breakup. Deep down, they didn't fully process the separation intentionally or unintentionally. The breakup wasn't born out of toxicity or incompatibility—it was driven by an internal panic or a need to escape before being left. Consequently, because abandonment, not wrongdoing, was the root cause, they find it hard or impossible to view their ex-partners harshly in a negative light.

These women often struggle to articulate why they left in the first place. That inability to explain is a red flag—not of confusion, but of an emotional blind spot. It clearly shows they cannot acknowledge the deeper issue: they need help. It does not help to find the one, but it helps to heal the pattern that causes them to *leave the one* prematurely.

Breaking the cycle of serial dating and emotional sabotage starts with such a level of self-awareness: abandonment is not just a feeling. It's a wound. And wounds don't close or heal on their own—they must be tended to with patience, therapy, and self-compassion.

Understanding these emotional triggers allows us to separate our past pain from present reality, leading to healthier responses rather than knee-jerk reactions.

Conflict Resolution: How We Argue and Heal

Relationship conflict isn't just about the issue at hand—it's about how we process and respond to emotional discomfort. Our emotional maps influence whether we shut down, lash out, seek reassurance, or try to fix things too quickly.

A person raised in an environment where conflict was avoided often struggles to communicate their needs openly. Instead of expressing themselves, they may suppress their feelings, fearing confrontation or dismissal. This tendency is prevalent in households with many siblings, where conversations can be loud, fast-paced, and competitive. Not everyone gets a turn to speak in such settings—especially those with quieter or more introspective personalities.

Introverted children, for example, may find it challenging to keep up with these dynamics. They need time to process their thoughts before speaking, but that space is rarely granted in a bustling household. Over time, they may internalize the belief that their voice doesn't matter—or that silence is safer than the risk of being ignored or misunderstood.

Consider a young girl growing up in a house full of outspoken, assertive male siblings. The boys may naturally dominate conversations, argue easily, and challenge one another openly. Being softer spoken, she might find herself constantly talked over; her voice drowned out in the noise.

Without guidance or encouragement from caregivers to create emotional balance, she may grow up feeling emotionally submerged, unduly submissive, or grow up without a 'voice.' In adulthood, this can manifest as her reluctance to speak up in relationships. She might struggle to state her needs, avoid expressing dissatisfaction, or default to people-pleasing behaviors—just to keep the peace.

This pattern doesn't stem from weakness but from conditioning. Her emotional map was formed in an environment that didn't allow her the room to develop confident self-expression, autonomy, or free will. As a result, unless she actively works to unlearn this pattern, she may carry it into romantic relationships, friendships, or even professional spaces, fully feeling seen or heard.

Recognizing these differences helps couples approach conflict with empathy, realizing that their partner's reaction isn't necessarily about them but about their emotional history. A couple can choose to love, exercise patience, and treat each other with the understanding that they have different emotional maps. Still, those maps converge through a wave of growth. Such a support system and sounding board of encouragement from each other will procure love and light rather than judgment, reprimand, chastisement, or belittlement.

Emotional Baggage vs. Emotional Wisdom

Not all emotional maps lead us astray—some provide truly valuable insight. Emotional experiences, both painful and joyful, shape how we show up in relationships. The key is distinguishing between emotional baggage (unprocessed wounds that hold us back) and emotional wisdom (lessons that help us grow).

Emotional baggage says: *"I was hurt before, so I can't trust anyone."*

This mindset develops as a form of self-protection. After experiencing pain, betrayal, or abandonment, the mind builds walls to prevent a repeat of the same suffering. While these defenses may feel necessary in the short term, they can distort a person's perception of others if left unchecked. Eventually, the victim may begin to believe that *everyone* means harm, leading to deep trust issues and emotional isolation.

Emotional wisdom, on the other hand, says: *"I was hurt before, so now I know how to recognize red flags and set healthy boundaries."*

This is the outcome of doing the inner work—of healing past wounds, reconciling childhood and relationship trauma, and transforming pain into discernment. Emotional wisdom doesn't deny past hurt—it learns from it. It doesn't build walls. It builds filters.

Rather than approaching life with suspicion and fear, emotional wisdom brings a renewed, positive outlook. It fosters healthier relationships because it's no longer operating from a place of fear but from a place of awareness and strength.

The shift from baggage to wisdom transforms emotional survival into emotional freedom. When partners work to understand their emotional maps, they can create a relationship where they feel seen, heard, and supported rather than controlled by past wounds and emotional limitations.

Healing and Building New Pathways

The beautiful thing about emotional maps is that they aren't set in stone. If we seek to... we can *redraw* them. We do so by creating healthier pathways for love, trust, and connection. But the first step in that journey begins with *looking inward*, often by revisiting our childhood and early formative years.

It likewise starts with recognizing a powerful truth: by the time we reach adulthood, especially after age 20—most of what we experience in life is either a repetition of something we've already lived through or been exposed to through others.

Our interpretations of the world are profoundly shaped by what we've been taught, seen, and emotionally anchored to.

Take the idea or romantic gesture involving roses, for example. In some parts of the world, roses don't even hold a romantic value. They are simply flowers. In some countries, roses don't grow naturally in their environment or regional habitat and hold no symbolic meaning. However, in the West—particularly in the United States—roses have become the *unofficial flower of love*. Consider how many roses are purchased on Valentine's Day alone.

Here's the surprising part: couples have broken up over roses' absence on Valentine's Day. Why? Because, at some point, society gave roses emotional significance. They became a *symbol* of love, not because the flower itself holds an emotion, but because we attached an emotion *to* it.

A rose, in reality, is a trimmed flower from a thorny plant. It has no feelings or emotions. But it becomes a symbol of love and an emotional expression to someone who associates it with love—perhaps because they saw their parents exchange roses or a first love gifted them a rose.

So, if a woman values roses deeply, she must pause and ask herself: *Why?* Where did that emotional association come from? Did her caregivers model it? Was it shaped by romantic movies, cultural norms, or childhood memories? Without this awareness, she may reject genuine acts of love *simply* because they don't come in the form of a rose.

Here's an even deeper question: *Is Valentine's Day the only day she should feel loved?* Of course not—it would seem irrational to believe so. And yet, a single flower—or the lack thereof—can threaten the foundation of a viable and amazing relationship, all because of an unexamined emotional map and society's capitalistic impediment to the couple's intrinsic bond.

As mentioned, this is why self-reflection is very important and is key. Revisiting the past isn't about blame—it's about curiosity. It's about asking *why* we value certain things more than others and where those ideas originated. Only by doing this can we create new, more balanced emotional pathways.

Understanding your partner's emotional patterns—and weighing them against your own—helps you better navigate emotional triggers and communication breakdowns. This doesn't mean defending your perspective at all costs. It means inquiring: *Why does this matter so much to me? And why doesn't it matter to him in the same way?*

Healthy relationships grow when two people commit to understanding one another beyond their surface-level behaviors and emotional histories. Open conversations about fears, needs, expectations, and triggers create safety. Seeking therapy, pursuing healing, and sharing honestly are the first true steps toward *redrawing your emotional map.*

Dating and relationships are less about finding the perfect partner and more about learning to explore emotional landscapes together. When two people bring awareness to their emotional maps, they can create a relationship built on mutual understanding, compassion, and growth. Instead of being ruled by the past, they can chart a new course that leads to lasting love and emotional fulfillment.

Chapter 5

How Dysfunctional Relationships Start

They start in our childhood.

Now that we understand how our developmental stages shape us, it becomes clear that any missteps—whether caused by negligence, trauma, or unintentional ignorance from our primary caregivers—can result in the dysfunctional or toxic traits we carry into adulthood. These traits don't just appear out of nowhere. The conflicts we experience in relationships, workplaces, and communities often have roots in the earliest years of our lives.

Let me be clear: it is entirely possible that your perception of a former partner—no matter how negative your experience with him may have been—doesn't tell the whole story. You may have played a more significant role in the dysfunction than you're willing to admit.

I know that's a difficult pill to swallow. Even entertaining the idea may stir up innate defensiveness, justifiable discomfort, or our outright resistance. But here's the truth: if reading that made you tense, angry, or uneasy, that reaction is actually a *clue*. It's a signal that there may be an *unhealed part of you*—a place that still carries pain, blame, or unresolved emotion.

And that leads to an important question:

Have you ever wondered why therapists are so interested in your childhood?

Therapists focus on childhood experiences because those emotional developmental stages play a crucial role in shaping your thoughts, emotional maps, behaviors, and how you relate to others in adulthood. The foundation of who we are, how we handle success or failure, stressful situations, and how we communicate with others is created in our childhood.

Our childhood?

Our childhood shapes our emotional and mental patterns. How we were treated as children when we were younger truly affects our self-esteem, emotional strength, and coping skills. If we grew up feeling safe and loved, we are more likely to develop healthy emotional regulation. If we experienced neglect, abuse, criticism, or trauma, we may struggle with anxiety, depression, or trust issues later in life. So, do you feel anxious, depressed, or have trust issues? We will discuss how these issues from your childhood may be sabotaging your relationships.

By zealously examining our childhood experiences, we can understand our modern-day attachment styles as adults or how we bond with others. This is because our first bonding relationship happens with our primary caregivers or parents.

How our parents bonded with us is vital in bonding with our loved ones. Could it be possible for us to keep breaking up with suitable men because of our attachment styles? Do we even know our attachment styles? More on that later. For now, we must understand that those secure attachments in childhood lead to healthy relationships. At the same time, inconsistent or absent caregiving can result in the fear of intimacy, dependency, or avoidance in relationships.

Do you fear or avoid intimacy? Is your partner likely to complain that the relationship is void of intimacy?

When unresolved early childhood issues are not dealt with, they lead to fears, insecurities, and negative behaviors later on in life, specifically in one's relationships. For example, women who struggle with a fear of being abandoned may have had an emotionally unavailable parent growing up. The caregiver did not establish security through consistent presence. As a result, the child developed a fear of being abandoned.

Suppose your parents left you hungry, crying for far too long without attention, and or didn't cuddle you for reassurance as often as humanly possible. In that case, you will likely fear that your partner will eventually abandon you the same way your mother or caregiver did. Why does this matter? It matters because by understanding our childhood, we can discover the issues affecting our daily lives, break those cycles through therapy and positive reassurance, and heal from negative emotional maps.

Childhood trauma—whether through neglect, emotional or physical abuse, or instability—often lays the foundation for self-sabotaging behaviors later in life. These behaviors are not random; they are protective mechanisms formed in response to early emotional wounds.

For example, if you were emotionally neglected as a child, being *ignored* in a relationship might feel familiar, even strangely safe. But when a partner shows consistent care, attentiveness, and emotional closeness, it may feel intrusive or overwhelming. Subconsciously, you associate their closeness with a loss of autonomy, freedom, smothering, or even danger. As a result, you may push them away—not because they've done something wrong, but because *closeness* feels threatening. You only feel safe when there's emotional distance.

On the surface, this might seem like you're just "protecting your peace" or maintaining your boundaries, yet, in truth, it's a learned coping mechanism that ends up sabotaging a connection. Suppose you're unaware of this pattern or quickly apprised of your behaviors. In that case, you'll likely conclude that your partner is at fault for the breakup. You'll see the end of the relationship as *their* failure to understand you—not as a reflection of your unhealed wounds.

This brings us back to my earlier point: your ex-lover might not be the villain in your story. The perception you held at the time may have been filtered through unhealed pain.

If you choose not to do the internal work—if you avoid therapy, ignore self-reflection, or resist accountability—then the generational cycles of emotional disappointment and broken relationships will continue. They won't end with you.

To cope without healing, many women adopt defense mechanisms like emotional withdrawal, avoidance, or even aggression. These behaviors may offer temporary relief but come at the cost of lasting love and emotional intimacy. True healing requires more than coping—it requires *transformation*.

A therapist can help pinpoint the origin of a strong emotional reaction, and they can also help you *process* it more effectively. In essence, they help you give that experience *meaning*. Understanding where a reaction comes from allows you to respond with clarity rather than confusion, hurt, pain, denial, or unnecessary defensiveness.

Take, for example, a romantic relationship where you suddenly find yourself avoiding physical intimacy or craving emotional distance. If you genuinely care for this person, why do you feel resentment or discomfort around their closeness to you?

That's the moment to pause and scan your emotional map. Ask yourself: *Was I emotionally close to my parents growing up? Was affection modeled in healthy ways? Did I feel safe opening up emotionally?*

Unless we revisit our childhood experiences, we cannot correct the patterns in our present. Some of us grew up in homes with inconsistent or absent emotional connections. Others faced emotional neglect, lacked nurturing support, or experienced deeper emotional wounds that never fully healed. These early imprints created our emotional maps—the internal blueprints influencing how we engage with love, intimacy, and connection.

So when dysfunction shows up in relationships, we must resist the urge to believe that *we are fine and that our partner is the problem*. That mindset only delays healing. Accountability is essential. Suppose we're participating in a dysfunctional relationship. In that case, we have to be willing to ask ourselves: *How am I contributing to this?*

Because no matter how things unfold, one truth always remains: it takes two to tango.

Negative Relationship Behaviors Linked to Early Childhood Development

Fear of Abandonment – You feel insecure and want to be clingy to your mate. This means that in your childhood, you experienced inconsistent caregiving, frequent separations, or an absentee parent or caregiver. Growing up, you fear being abandoned. In relationships, you become overly needy, jealous, or anxious when your partner is unavailable, constantly seeking reassurance that you won't be left. You think about breakups so often that sometimes you want to be preemptive to feel more secure.

If you break up with him first, you'll feel better than being caught unaware. Loneliness and abandonment overpower the feelings of being in a relationship. The likely outcome for women stuck in this cycle is to end up dating multiple partners for security while continually sabotaging relationships. Often, these women have difficulty describing what was wrong in their previous relationships.

Difficulty Expressing Emotions – You experience difficulties in expressing your emotions. You, therefore, withdraw from your partner or avoid communicating. As a child, you were raised in an environment where emotions were dismissed, ignored, or punished, so you quickly learned to suppress your feelings. Therefore, as an adult, you struggle to communicate how you feel in relationships, and you find yourself shutting down during conflicts or avoiding deep emotional connections out of fear of being judged or rejected.

Fear of Rejection – You avoid telling others your boundaries out of the fear of adverse reaction. In other words, you want to please people at your own expense, no matter how painful. This lack of boundaries stems from your childhood. As a child, you were only praised when you pleased or made others happy but were criticized when you expressed your desires and needs if they did not align with your caregiver's desires and needs. This developed a fear of disappointing people. As an adult in relationships, you may have difficulty setting boundaries, so you say "yes" to things you don't want and avoid conflict to keep your partner happy—often at your own expense.

***Controlling Behavio*r** – You have a burning desire to be in control and need power in relationships. In your childhood, you grew up in an unpredictable or chaotic household. To feel safe, you adopt the need to control others to secure internal peace. As an adult in a relationship, you try to control your partner's actions, choices, or emotions because you fear losing control will result in instability, hurt, or break up.

Difficulty Trusting Others – You feel like competing with unknown people trying to take your partner. You experience rage and are not good enough if your partner gets attention from any woman other than you. Even if it is in business or socially acceptable gesture or compliment. Your level of jealousy and suspicion is sometimes unfounded, but it still feels authentic to you. As a child, you were frequently lied to, manipulated, or let down by caregivers, and so you struggled to trust people. As an adult in relationships, you may become overly suspicious, jealous, or assume the worst, even when there's no real reason for doubt.

Avoiding Commitment – You fear being intimate; closeness with your partner makes you uncomfortable. As a child, you experienced neglect, and your caregiver was emotionally distanced from you (a form of avoidant attachment), and that lack of affection led you to associate closeness with pain, disappointment, or eventual loss. As an adult, you keep partners at a distance; this behavior leads to sabotaging relationships in many cases before they even get serious, or you directly avoid deep emotional connections.

Aggressive or Explosive Reactions – You have difficulty managing conflict. You feel like you must stand your ground all the time. Even in explicit situations where it is evident you may be wrong. Managing conflicts or misunderstandings is your weakness; things always escalate into breakups, physical fights, and verbal confrontations that cause scenes and stir your communities. Running in with the law is synonymous with your anger explosion during conflicts. As a child, you were raised in a home with frequent arguments, yelling, or physical punishment. You learned that aggression is the only way to handle conflict. As an adult in relationships, you may respond to disagreements with anger, shouting, or even shutting down rather than working through issues calmly.

Over-Attachment or Dependency – You over-rely on your partner for emotional stability. You need to settle your anxieties and insecurities; sometimes, you want to regulate your emotions. As a child, you were overly coddled, sheltered, and not encouraged to be independent, so as an adult, you struggle with self-reliance. In relationships, you may rely too much on your partner for validation, decision-making, and emotional support, making you uncomfortable to function independently.

Chapter 6

How Women Experience Love Through Emotions

Emotions play a powerful role in a woman's experience of love. While the brain processes attraction and logic, emotions give those thoughts meaning. When you see an attractive man, your brain recognizes his looks, but it's your emotions that create feelings of excitement and connection. As a woman, you rely more on emotions when choosing a partner because your love is deeply felt, not just understood.

For example, you might say, *"I feel he loves me."* This feeling is not just a thought—it comes from his actions. You interpret his words, gestures, and attention through your emotions to decide whether he genuinely cares about you. Equally, a simple hug from a friend feels different from a hug from someone you love because emotions always add depth to the connection.

As a woman, you also have a natural and intuitive ability to sense emotions in relationships. You pick up on small changes in his tone, body language, or behavior, helping you determine whether his love is genuine. Your emotions act as an internal guide of discernment, giving you invaluable clues about whether a relationship is strong and genuine or uncertain and unsteady.

Emotions, however, can sometimes cloud judgment. When deeply in love, you may overlook serious warning signs (red flags) or excuse prior typically non-negotiable behaviors because of how you feel. You might believe a man loves you, even when his actions say otherwise. This emotional connection is also why breakups can be especially painful—you are not just losing a person but also the deep feelings and memories tied to him, and in many ways, you feel like you are losing or mourning the loss or the death of a best friend.

Love, attraction, and commitment come from how you feel in a relationship. A man's words might sound nice, but your emotions will eventually sense the difference if his actions do not match. You seek emotional security, and when you feel safe, valued, and cherished, you open your heart completely.

Mastering Emotions: The Key to a Healthy Relationship

Since emotions shape how we experience love, we must learn to *master* them—through awareness, reflection, and intention. One way to do this is by creating a mental *sequence* that allows us to process emotional responses, especially when it comes to attraction.

The next time you see a man and feel instantly drawn to him, pause for a moment and ask yourself a few key questions:

1. Why is this man attractive to me?
2. What specifically about him makes me feel that way?
3. Who or what taught me that a man with those particular traits is considered attractive?

These simple yet powerful questions interrupt emotional autopilots and invite *self-awareness and self-respect.*

Once you've answered them, the next step is to ask yourself: *What should I do with this feeling of attraction?* Is it worth exploring? Or is it just a surface-level spark tied to an old pattern or emotional trigger?

This sequencing of thought—asking and answering with honesty—can save you from heartache and disappointment down the road.

We all can agree that emotions are beautiful. They bring excitement to new relationships, help sustain long-term connections, and guide us in discerning whether someone's love is real or not. But when unfiltered and unexamined, emotions can lead us into situations we regret later. Without sequencing or reflection, many women find themselves in intimate situations with men who, on the surface, seemed ideal—but later revealed deeper dysfunctions, even more damaging than their previous partners.

That's why *emotional depth* and self-awareness are essential for building strong, lasting relationships. Attraction is natural, but maturity lies in understanding *why* we're attracted to a specific person—and whether that attraction leads us toward love or another critical life lesson.

At first glance, this might seem simple—after all, experiencing emotions in love typically feels natural. But if emotions alone were enough to lead you to the right partner, why has finding *Mr. Right* been so difficult? And suppose emotions were meant to protect your heart, then why haven't they shielded you from painful breakups, toxic relationships, or the disappointment that often follows dating?

Powerful emotions can also be *misleading* if not correctly understood or interpreted. Many women unknowingly allow their feelings to take the lead and grab the reigns without questioning the direction they're heading in. This emotional autopilot ultimately leads ... 'not' to the sought-after happiness, leaving the individual aimlessly searching for ... but instead ends up in an inevitable heartbreak.

It's worth remembering that *"just because you feel something doesn't mean you need to act on it. Just because you want to say something doesn't mean you should."*

Emotions are *fleeting*. They are like the weather—constantly shifting. A forecast that says "partly cloudy" could mean patches of sun, brief showers, or overcast skies. It's not one or the other; it's a mix—and so are emotions. Just because today feels dark doesn't mean tomorrow will not bring clarity and light.

So, when a woman makes a long-term, major decision in a temporary emotional and short-lived state of despair—whether it is to end a relationship, cut someone off, or jump into something new—*based solely on how she feels in the moment.*

She risks when making choices based on emotions that may change once the smoke clears.

A bad day shouldn't warrant a life-altering decision to be made.

The lesson here is *emotional mindfulness* and control. Women must be aware that decisions made in the heat of emotional intensity are rarely stable. As emotions shift, so do perspectives. Being mindful doesn't mean ignoring your feelings—it means pausing long enough to examine them before letting them dictate your next move or determine the irretrievable words that will come out of your mouth next.

This is why we need to go beyond the surface level of how emotions feel and how they actually function. While this may seem psychological or scientific, mastering these insights will change how we approach love and relationships. By understanding how our emotions can build and sabotage connections, we can use them wisely to secure a fulfilling relationship.

Emotions generally fall into two categories: *basic emotions* and *complex emotions.*

Basic emotions—such as happiness, sadness, anger, fear, surprise, and disgust—are universal and instinctive. They are hardwired into the human experience and appear across all cultures. These emotions are quick, automatic responses to situations, often without conscious thought.

Complex emotions, on the other hand, include feelings like love, guilt, jealousy, shame, and pride. These emotions are shaped by biology and personal experiences, upbringing, values, and social conditioning. They tend to be layered, contradictory, and more complex to interpret.

This is why many women find it challenging to understand their *true* feelings when they are in love. One moment, they may feel overwhelming excitement—even sexual attraction—and the next, a wave of uncertainty or emotional withdrawal. These emotional swings aren't simple; they're *complex*, so they can feel confusing and sometimes paralyzing.

When a woman is unsure about how she feels and what she should do about those feelings—it's important to resist the urge to act impulsively. A simple but powerful rule to follow is:

When you're uncertain, don't act or speak prematurely.

This moment of stillness creates room for clarity. It's a way of emotionally regulating ourselves, especially when navigating complex emotions that can cloud judgment and influence high-stakes decisions.

Take, for example, the reality that a majority of divorces are initiated by women, often citing emotional dissatisfaction or unhappiness. While many of those decisions may be valid, it's worth considering how many could be reconsidered if the women involved paused—*just for a moment*—to reflect deeper.

This is not to suggest that all divorces should be avoided, but rather to emphasize the importance of stepping back and evaluating whether the emotional dissatisfaction is rooted in consistent patterns of neglect or harm—or if it's tied to temporary emotional discontent that could shift with time, healing, or communication.

Complex emotions require *discernment*. And discernment takes *time*.

Mastering emotions in love is not just about feeling; it's about understanding and using emotions to strengthen, rather than weaken, a woman's journey to true love, to avoid her treating her partner or suitor arbitrarily or capriciously.

Love is not just spoken but shown in how we hold, touch, and look at the ones who mean the most to us. These outward expressions of emotion—whether a lingering hug, a stolen glance, or how our voices soften when we say their name—are the truest language of the heart.

The Power of Emotions in Relationships

Emotions constantly shape your thoughts, actions, and interactions in a relationship. Just as you instinctively react to a loud noise or slowly develop trust in something over time, meaningful relationships follow a similar process. Strong, lasting love does not happen overnight—just like Rome wasn't built in a day, and neither should your relationship. If you want it to last, you must allow it to grow naturally and steadily.

Understanding how emotions function in a relationship is, therefore, fundamental. They have the power to either strengthen your bond or create unnecessary conflict. When correctly managed, emotions can promote trust, intimacy, and connection.

However, if left unchecked, emotions can lead women to react impulsively and volatile during minuscule disagreements with their significant others. Recognizing and controlling emotions can help women navigate love with clarity, poise, and integrity while ensuring their relationship is built on a strong foundation rather than fleeting feelings.

But how exactly do emotions work? To master them, we must break down their unique composition. Every emotion follows a natural cycle, and by understanding each phase, we can choose how to react—or even stop an emotion from running its full course.

For example, imagine someone accidentally bumping into you at a crowded shopping mall. Your immediate reaction might be irritation or even anger. This is a *basic emotional response*—a quick instinct triggered by surprise or perceived intrusion.

Depending on your temperament, you might glare at them, snap back in frustration, or mutter under your breath. Someone with a higher propensity for aggression may not respond the same way. They may choose confrontation, while calmer individuals may frown and move on.

But then you turn around and notice something you didn't expect—the person has a limp, a cane, is blind, or has a visible disability. In an instant, your anger softens, replaced by understanding, even compassion, and you instantly feel ashamed of how quickly you were to 'anger.' Maybe they even go as far as to apologize to you, and suddenly, the frustration that once felt justified now feels unnecessary and dissipates.

This shift highlights something essential: *the power of the pause.*

Had you reacted without taking that brief moment to reassess, your response might have escalated an innocent encounter into an unnecessary conflict—something you may have later regretted.

This ability to *pause before reacting* is a skill, not a weakness. It's one of the most valuable tools we can use in our relationships—romantic, professional, or otherwise.

Giving ourselves just a few seconds to gather perspective allows empathy and wisdom to step in before emotions take control.

In relationships, this pause can especially prevent arguments, misunderstandings, and the damage that impulsive words or actions often cause. It's not about suppressing emotions but about managing them with maturity. Doing so will avoid sabotaging your relationships, especially those you genuinely want to nurture.

Chapter 7

The Accountability Question

Now that you understand how emotions are formed and how childhood experiences shape your emotional roadmap, it becomes clear why self-reflection, healing from past pain, and overcoming discouragement are essential for cultivating meaningful relationships. Building a healthy partnership begins with internal awareness and emotional maturity.

We've also explored how romanticized ideals, social conditioning, and the evolution of modern dating have shaped expectations—often blurring the line between what we *want* and what we *actually need*. With this foundational understanding in place, it's time to confront one of the most overlooked yet critical aspects of a woman's relationship journey: **the art of accountability.**

Before we examine *the '5' types of men every woman chooses from*, we must pause and address a truth many women struggle to face: **that you can't choose or keep the right man if you're unwilling to take ownership of your relationship patterns.**

Both men and women struggle with accountability—but *why is that?*

At the root of accountability lies a sobering possibility: upon closer examination, we may be *at fault* or *in error*. That realization is very uncomfortable for some. To protect our egos, we often deflect blame, justify our behavior, or even lash out in anger at the mere suggestion that we hold some responsibility for an action or statement of ours.

Accountability shines a light into the deepest corners of the soul—the places many would rather keep hidden. And in that light, many people feel exposed. Vulnerable. Seen.

That's why, in today's culture, we often see a different response: deflection dressed up as storytelling. Social media is now filled with videos and posts where individuals accuse, shame, or berate former partners. The narrative is one-sided, painting them as the innocent party and their ex as the villain. What's often *left out* of those stories is the one question they desperately avoid: **Why did they choose that relationship in the first place?**

That single question changes the entire focus. It shifts the spotlight from the partner's behavior to *the chooser's judgment*. And for many, that kind of introspection is too uncomfortable. Not because their ex didn't do anything wrong—but because facing that question means acknowledging a truth they'd rather avoid: *that they were equally part of the equation, too.*

Now, let's be absolutely clear—this particular segment of the conversation that will be discussed in this chapter does not include the applications of these concepts when it involves abusive relationships, relationships that involve violations of anyone's safety, or relationships that lack consent. It is very important to note and always to remember that victims or survivors of any sort (especially those concerning children, protected classes of people, and any other vulnerable individuals), must never be blamed for the harm inflicted upon them. Unlawfully salacious and Predatory behavior is not only criminal but is truly reprehensible and is absolutely not included in all that we will discuss and address in this chapter.

Instead, this chapter will address concepts surrounding *consensual relationships*—where two adults enter a partnership and, over time, face traditional challenges such as arguments, disagreements, adultery, infidelity, financial irresponsibility, or emotional incompatibility. When these relationships end, one partner may shame the other publicly, spreading stories to friends, family, or even online audiences to preserve their image by tarnishing someone else's.

However, what often proves to be missing from those narratives is a conversation about *their own contribution* to the relationship. What red flags did they ignore? What needs were they trying to fill? What patterns have they repeated in past relationships?

Proper accountability doesn't ask, *"Who's to blame?"* It asks, *"What part did I play—and what can I learn from it?"*

The cycle will likely continue until we are honest with ourselves. No matter who we date next, we'll carry the same unexamined behaviors, beliefs, and blind spots—trading faces but repeating the same emotional script.

Accountability may be uncomfortable when it comes to ideas and the notions of love, but it is the bridge between *where you've been* and *where you want to be*

Accountability is more than admitting to ourselves when we are wrong—it is instead about being *honest* with ourselves. Why do we ignore red flags? Why do we choose emotionally unavailable men? Why do we stay in cycles of confusion or chase validation through chemistry that lacks substance?

Too often, women place the blame solely on the men: *"He changed," "He couldn't handle me,"* or *"These men nowadays just aren't serious anymore."* While there may be truth in some of these claims, they don't tell the whole story. At some point, the real question becomes: *Why did I choose him? What made me stay? And what part of me believed that's all I deserved?*

This is the uncomfortable yet necessary line of questioning we must ask ourselves, and ultimately, it is the work we must do if we want to see different results and internal growth within ourselves. Without accountability, we will likely choose the same type of partner under a different ruse or name.

Although love may often become a trial and error, creating disappointment after disappointment with accountability, we can reclaim our power. A reclaiming of power will not just *attract* the right partner but will also *sustain* a healthy and balanced relationship.

So, as we prepare to explore the *'5' men that every woman can undoubtedly choose from*, remember that *'Clarity begins with Courage,'* The courage required to be accountable on a higher level that will ultimately position you to not only love ... but to be loved.

As a woman, you can be intentional about the type of man you want in a long-term relationship. This isn't about being unaware of what you want; it means prioritizing your life, mental state and physical health, and future family. Become accountable if you care about growth and envision a loving, stable partnership that will last a lifetime.

As discussed in the previous chapters, external pressures often interfere with finding a compatible partner. Society, family, and friends frequently ask, "Why aren't you married yet?" or "Why haven't you met someone special?" For women who lack emotional awareness and self-confidence, these questions can create a sense of urgency, making it tempting to settle for someone who isn't the right fit.

The pressure to move quickly often leads to rushed decisions, resulting in unfulfilling relationships and long-term complications. However, for women who have done the self-reflection and healing work outlined earlier, the process becomes much smoother, and the outside noises of the world, family, and friends are just that ... noises. There's absolutely no need to rush or compromise oneself. Instead, it is imperative that you can move forward at your own pace with confidence, knowing that choosing wisely is far more important than choosing quickly.

People will always have opinions about your love life, but they won't walk in your shoes or make the bed you will lie in. This is your life, and you must take ownership of it courageously and unapologetically. You deserve to share it only with the right partner—not someone you settle for out of fear, duress, pressure, impatience, or insecurities.

Remember this: if you don't do the inner work, you risk repeating the same mistakes and wasting another opportunity for real love. True fulfillment comes from making intentional choices, not rushing into relationships to satisfy outside expectations. Take your time, trust the process, and choose wisely.

When choosing a man for a long-term relationship, ensuring he possesses qualities that support a stable and fulfilling partnership is essential.

Clear and Open Communication

Understanding each other with *minimal confusion* is essential in any lasting relationship. Whether he's feeling happy, frustrated, ambitious, or simply needing support, both partners should be able to communicate honestly and effectively. When expressing thoughts and emotions becomes a struggle, misunderstandings grow, and unnecessary tension begins to chip away at the foundation of the relationship.

Intimacy, at its core, should generally foster deeper awareness between partners. It's meant to be a safe space where both individuals can explore their unique qualities and desires without judgment. Sex, in this context, should not feel like a chore or obligation—but rather a shared experience born from emotional connection and passion.

When there's a depletion in romance, emotional connections, or physical closeness, couples should feel safe enough to talk about it—*without fear of rejection or punishment,* whether through silence, emotional distance, or passive-aggressive behaviors. This type of emotional safety is especially important for women to understand and practice if they want to build something lasting.

It's also vital to recognize that **many men don't intentionally set out to be unfaithful**. Often, infidelity stems from deeper emotional needs—such as the desire for validation—or it's a learned behavior from past relationship wounds. While cheating is never justified, it's important to explore *why* it even happens in the first place.

Women frequently express concerns about men cheating—which, in many cases, is valid and painful. But underneath the surface, many women unknowingly engage in **emotional cheating**. Here's the difference:

Men often seek **physical intimacy**, while women tend to crave **emotional connection**. Now, this is where things get complicated.

A woman may maintain emotionally close relationships with male friends she's not dating, receiving attention, validation, and comfort that should be cultivated within her primary relationship. When those emotional needs are met elsewhere, she may no longer feel the urgency or desire to connect physically with her partner—and that imbalance creates a silent distance between the two.

Culturally, we don't always view emotional intimacy with someone outside the relationship as betrayal. But emotional cheating is just as damaging—if not more so—because it undermines trust and connection from within and usurps the bond that the two people in the relationship were fostering and organically building.

While men may cheat physically first, women often cheat emotionally first, and the physical usually and often follows. This is why it is pertinent that women do the inner work—*before* seeking a long-term partner. Keeping emotional connections with male friends might seem harmless. Still, it only seeks to create blind spots and emotional dependencies that can sabotage even the healthiest of relationships. Without addressing this, knowing the *5 types of men* to choose from won't matter—because unhealed patterns will continue to appear.

Additionally, men, at their core, desire two fundamental things:

1. **Respect**—feeling seen, valued, and affirmed; and...
2. **Physical intimacy**—not just sex, but a connection that makes them feel wanted and accepted.

It doesn't matter which type of man a woman chooses from the '5' if *she does not do the work or genuinely desire the above-stated two fundamental needs, respect and physical intimacy, regardless of her finding a perfect match out of the 5 men, her relationship will be shortlived. She will struggle with offering genuine respect to her partner if she lacks physical attraction towards him or fails to participate in being transparently and emotionally open with him.* That relationship will be on shaky ground from its inception before it can take off and flourish.

This is why constant and open communication must be more than a good habit—it must be the *foundation*. When couples can speak freely about needs, fears, and expectations, they build emotional strength. They create a partnership where both feel secure enough to be vulnerable, assuring longevity and a more fulfilling life together.

Shared Values and Priorities

A relationship where both partners have opposing life goals often leads to conflict. For instance, if he loves to travel and explore while you thrive in a calm, home-centered life, this mismatch could cause ongoing friction. Aligning values, lifestyle, and long-term goals is as important as attraction and affection.

Any woman seeking a long-term relationship must first take the time to align her own desires and values *before* stepping into dating with serious intentions. Most relationship complications arise not from a lack of love but from a clash in vision. When two people's life paths are heading in different directions, the result is usually confusion, frustration, and emotional disconnect. At the core of these conflicts lies the inability—or unwillingness—to understand and respect each other's life goals.

To illustrate this, consider the infamous duo **Bonnie and Clyde**. While their story is often romanticized for its thrill and rebellion, one thing stands out: they were fully *aligned* in their mission—right or wrong. Bonnie Parker and Clyde Barrow shared a common purpose, common risks, and a common vision, and they rode together until the end. While their legacy is highly disturbing and their acts of crime committed completely egregious, we look only to the strength of their bond, which was built, however, unfortunately, on shared values and similar direction. They were partners—not just in crime—but in purpose and commitment, even throughout their acts of moral corruption and their crimes of moral turpitude.

Let's be clear that no one's suggesting you seek out a type of 'Bonnie and Clyde' type of love. Their love story, if you can even call it that, although criminals were still premised on aligning that powerful principle, they became unstoppable. The only lesson we can learn from them is that when two people are aligned in goals, values, and vision, it is impossible to break them apart. We see that these two clearly were sadistic in nature. Still, they vehemently protected each other's dreams and aspirations, unconditionally vested in each other's purpose, and walked hand-in-hand until the very end. Suppose they were good people in the community? Their lives could have been remembered as a great story of love. The point is that if a couple can align their values and core beliefs, unify their purpose, and be attracted to each other in love, that would be the perfect match.

As a woman, this is why it's so important to ask hard questions early on in dating and vetting the goals, intentions, beliefs, and prospects of your potential significant other. You must seek to find out ... What does he believe in? What drives him? What does he want five or ten years from now, and when you find out those answers, do those answers bring you peace ... or a semblance of anxiety?

Believe me, and you cannot walk in harmony with someone who is not aligned with you in terms of purpose and life. Love alone doesn't make a relationship work and move forward—*sheer alignment does.*

So, before you commit, make sure you're not just falling for 'chemistry' or falling in 'lust.' Search for clarity and look for shared values. When a relationship moves with the rhythm of mutual purpose, love doesn't have to fight to survive—it will grow naturally.

Single Parents

Dating intentionally as a single mother begins with clarity and boundaries. Her life is no longer just her own; she must protect the emotional environment she's built for her child. This doesn't mean she's disqualified from love—it simply means love must come with alignment.

She must be honest—with herself and with her dates—about what she's looking for, how her time is limited, and how sacred her role as a parent is. Instead of rushing to merge her worlds, she should take time to observe—how does he respond to responsibility? Is he patient with her schedule? Does he respect the pace at which she needs to move? Dating intentionally means not apologizing for being a mother but instead seeing it as a strength that filters out anyone who isn't ready for real commitment. Her heart can open again—but this time, with wisdom leading the way.

Younger Women

For the younger woman, intentional dating starts with *self-discovery*. Before she seeks love, she must take the time to explore who she is, what she values, and what she truly needs—not just what feels good in the moment. This is her season to set healthy standards and learn to say no without guilt. She must remind herself that being alone is not failure—it's preparation.

Instead of letting the pressure of peers or social media define her timeline, she can lean into learning what a real connection looks like. Intentionality for her means asking the deeper questions: *Does this person see me for who I am? Do I feel safe being vulnerable?* She must also guard her emotional energy and be careful not to give pieces of her heart to people who haven't earned her trust. Through reflection, boundaries, and honesty, she begins to date not for validation—but again for alignment.

Mature Women

The mature woman has the gift of hindsight and the ability to move with *grace and intention*. Her strength lies in her ability to be selective, not bitter, open, not desperate. Dating intentionally for her means embracing this new chapter with hope—not because she needs someone to complete her, but because she desires a partner who complements the life she's already built.

Thus, she must remain rooted in her truth, even if the world tells her to compromise for companionship. She can ask the hard questions early and walk away if the answers don't align with her values. It's not too late. Her love story doesn't need to look like anyone else's. Whether she finds someone new or chooses to remain centered in her journey, the point is not to settle—but to connect with someone who sees and cherishes the full, layered woman she has become.

No matter her age or her stage of life—whether it is balancing motherhood, stepping into womanhood, or walking with maturity, the key to intentional dating is *self-awareness*. When a woman understands her value, knows her patterns, and chooses not to be guided solely by emotion, she shifts from hoping love works out to *choosing love very wisely*.

Real love doesn't rush. It doesn't breed or blossom in places of confusion. And it certainly doesn't require losing oneself to obtain it.

Are You Ready for a Relationship?

Before entering the dating world, it's important to pause and ask yourself: Are you truly ready? Many women move quickly from one relationship to another without taking time to reflect and heal from past experiences. This behavior is often learned, driven by the need for companionship, societal expectations, or simply avoiding the discomfort of being alone.

One common mistake is confiding in others about relationship struggles instead of addressing issues directly with a partner or licensed professional. Although seeking advice from friends and family may seem like an inviting or enticing option when wanting to get practical advice about a life matter, unfortunately, we have seen over and over again that it can do more harm than good.

On the other hand, taking steps to seek out an impartial professional therapist or a neutral advisor to better provide you with the invaluable guidance you'll need will prove unarbitrary and unbiased, unlike that of our loved ones, whose advice more often than not will be laden with very biased and sometimes unsolicited opinions, judgments, feedback and misleading recommendations to your relationship challenges or peril.

As discussed, it is important to remember that due to everyone's subjective emotional mapping, the opinions of our loved ones may sometimes be inherently skewed because they are laden with their personal views, lived experiences, and their emotional connections or lack thereof with others. This is the formula for a disaster or a perfect storm. This is what you don't want. Taking heed to relationship advice that someone dear to you may advise you to do does not make you immune from the irreparable and final damage to your relationship and the irrevocability of your actions premised on your following their advice.

Bound by family loyalty, relatives may instinctively take your side rather than help you see the bigger picture. Similarly, but even worse, friends, on the other hand, might encourage you to make decisions that keep you within their social circle rather than deciding what would truly be best for you and your relationship. Sometimes, so-called friends may even secretly judge or make light of your repeated breakups and reconciliations rather than giving honest, constructive advice.

The Negative Impact of Seeking Advice from Wrong Sources

When someone frequently shares relationship troubles with friends who lack objectivity and neutrality, the advice given is often reactionary rather than thoughtful or even dire and destructive rather than discerning.

Some female friends may tell a woman to walk away without considering whether the relationship could have been effectively repaired through communication and effort. If these 'friends' genuinely cared, they would encourage the woman to seek professional help or spiritual guidance rather than reinforcing frivolous, impulsive, and permanent decisions.

Women should likewise be mindful of passive encouragement from friends, which only seeks to reinforce unhealthy patterns and stagnation counterproductively. If a friend constantly and consistently struggles to maintain healthy and viable relationships, the best way to support them is by urging self-reflection and professional guidance instead of enabling destructive cycles and reinforcing roadblocks.

If relationships repeatedly fail, at some point, it becomes necessary to examine the role one plays in these outcomes. It's not always about choosing the wrong partner—personal patterns and unresolved issues sometimes contribute to relationship struggles.

Ultimately, a true friend doesn't just agree or sympathize with you. A good friend should offer perspective and encourage accountability when enduring seasons of strife and challenges.

Questions to Consider Before Seeking External Advice From Others

- Am I looking for validation or real guidance?

- Is the person I'm confiding in genuinely objective, or are they simply agreeing with me?

- Have I taken time to reflect on my own role in my relationships before seeking outside opinions?

The Difference Between Fear-Based Dating and 'Monkey Branching'

'Monkey branching' is a term used to describe individuals who jump from one relationship to another in search of a wealthier or higher-status partner. Although these patterns might seem to resemble one another in definition and in similarity—the motivations for why women participate in fear-based dating and monkey branching substantially differ.

Women who monkey branch do so strategically, seeking to "trade up" to someone with more financial resources, assets, and wealth. The woman's behavior is thus driven by status and financial security, often influenced by family or social conditioning.

On the other hand, women who date multiple partners due to insecurity are women who are driven by emotional fear rather than material gain. Eventually, their need to avoid loneliness overrides their ability to form stable, committed relationships. In these cases, professional therapy or self-work is crucial to breaking the cycle and addressing their deep-seated fear of abandonment.

The Illusion of the Fairytale Wedding

Another common emotional trap is the obsession with weddings as an end goal. While there is nothing wrong with desiring a wedding, many women romanticize weddings rather than preparing for the marriage after the wedding.

As discussed earlier, romanticism creates unrealistic expectations, leading to extravagant ceremonies, unnecessary debt, and, in many cases, a quick divorce when reality sets in. A wedding is not the finish line—it is the starting point of a lifelong partnership that requires effort, patience, and flexibility.

Emotional Maturity

Marriage and long-term commitment are not just about finding the right person—they require personal growth and accountability. Without self-awareness, individuals may repeat unhealthy patterns, leading to a cycle of failed relationships and emotional distress.

Taking the time to heal, reflect, and develop emotional stability before entering a new relationship leads to healthier, more fulfilling partnerships. Challenges will always arise, but those who have done the internal work are better equipped to navigate them rather than running away at the first sign of difficulty.

Entering a Relationship for the Right Reasons

A relationship should never be pursued solely for the idea of protection or for financial security and sustainability. While financial stability and material gifts may be appealing, they certainly do not equate to emotional fulfillment.

For example, a wealthy man may shower you with gifts or grand gestures—but if he does the same for multiple women, does that truly make you feel valued? Meaningful relationships are built on genuine connection, emotional support, and mutual commitment.

Choosing the right partner isn't about what he can provide materially—it's about the life you can build together. Taking time for self-reflection and making thoughtful choices ensures that you enter relationships from a place of confidence and clarity rather than urgency or external pressure.

It is impossible to know a man's personality when you meet him. Still, you can quickly recognize incompatibility during initial conversations. The mistake many women make is believing they must act promptly to avoid wasting time. Still, the truth is that choosing a poorly matched partner wastes more time than waiting for someone genuinely compatible.

When you commit, you invest emotional energy, time, and effort. If the relationship turns unhealthy or even abusive, the process of undoing that choice becomes even more complicated.

Healing from heartbreak or trauma—especially if you don't seek therapy—can take years, further delaying your ability to build a healthy, fulfilling relationship.

Women should aim to identify men who align with their values and desires while allowing others to remain casual acquaintances. Too often, women turn small connections into significant relationships without assessing whether they are compatible. By being intentional in this process, they save time, avoid unnecessary heartbreak, and prevent broken families, divorces, and single parenthood due to a lack of commitment from a partner.

Imagine carrying a thousand dollars in cash with no wallet, purse, or security—just holding it out in the open while walking through a busy, high-crime area. If someone snatches your money out of your hand and runs away, the average person will ask you: Why in the world would you walk around that neighborhood with your cash exposed? And rightfully so.

The above analogy is not truly about whether you should be allowed to have the one thousand dollars in your possession ... just as it's not about whether you 'should seek'... love, intimacy, and connections with a partner. It is really about whether or not you have sought to qualify this new person or potential significant other with whom you are voluntarily choosing to become vulnerable. Vulnerability, in this case, is the cash in hand. When women are vulnerable, they predispose themselves to predatory men. That's how unwanted pregnancies, sexually transmitted diseases, and other unpleasant situations happen.

We often say we didn't know a relationship would turn out like it did. But that also means we lacked the proper criteria to assess whether someone was a good partner. That's the part of the conversation that demands accountability and actually looking within oneself.

If you find yourself in a cycle of breakups and cyclical disappointments in relationships, ask yourself: What is within me that keeps drawing me toward these experiences? That question is the first step toward healing.

For example, some men are naturally responsible. If an unexpected situation arises, such as raising a child together, some men prioritize fatherhood regardless of the relationship status. Others will not. When you learn to recognize these distinctions early on, you won't have to carry the weight of uncertainty or regret.

Likewise, some men are deeply committed, while others are not. Regardless of the type of man you prefer, the real question is: does he possess the qualities of commitment? This is where accountability comes in. External factors—such as financial stability, physical appearance, or social status—may influence attraction. Still, they do not determine the longevity of a relationship.

While it's natural to appreciate good looks and financial security, these aspects alone do not build lasting relationships. If that were the case, every wealthy and attractive couple would live a happily-ever-after story. Yet, we know that isn't true. Why? Because they were not truly aligned.

Financial success does not mean someone has the emotional maturity, values, or character necessary for a long-term relationship. Modern dating often confuses achievement with relationship readiness. A man's ability to provide financially does not necessarily mean he is ready or willing to give emotionally.

Consider this: a successful man built his wealth without you. When you enter a relationship with him, his perspective may not align with yours. You might see him as solely a provider, but he may see you as an additional expense or financial burden. He has likely structured his finances to minimize losses, which could include avoiding unnecessary spending—even on a partner. This could mean he hesitates to invest in things you consider natural in a committed relationship, such as buying a home or supporting shared expenses.

On the other hand, a man who grows with you—who becomes successful alongside you—naturally sees you as part of his journey. Whether he has ten dollars or a million, his desire to provide for you is rooted in love, not just obligation and begrudged duty. This is a critical difference: an emotionally invested man will give because he wants to, not because he feels pressured to.

Beyond Physical Attraction

Good looks fade with time. A 24-year-old woman will not look the same at 54, even with the best efforts to preserve youth. While cosmetic procedures may enhance features, they do not stop the natural progression of aging. The truth is, if someone views aging as unattractive, they are rejecting the inevitable course and circle of life.

A man who loves you does not need external modifications to remain attracted to you. His attraction is based on a more profound and integral connection—embedded in the essence of who you are, your values, and the bond you share.

When you meet a man, he will almost seamlessly and organically align with your priorities—but only if you genuinely know your priorities. It's essential to differentiate between genuine priorities and reactive decisions driven by fear. Saying, "I'm getting older, so I better find someone," is not a priority; it's panic.

It's important to note that panic only leads to rushed decisions and dire and/or life-altering unwanted consequences.

Remember, as you move forward in your relationship journey and self-growth, nothing good comes from desperation, anxiety, or moving too fast. Speed doesn't beget or guarantee the success of one's goals. If something seems too good to be true, remember that it is most often true. Seek wisdom and always use discernment in all things and at all times.

Another common mistake to avoid is immediately discussing marriage with a man shortly after meeting him. This signals that you are more interested in marriage than in the person himself. Men are not blind; they are not without intuition or feelings.

They know that many women only romanticize weddings and relationships without fully considering what it takes to sustain them.

Think of it like winning the lottery. People who suddenly acquire large sums of money often lose it because they lack the financial discipline to manage it. The same applies to relationships. If you struggle with personal accountability, communication, or emotional stability, entering a relationship won't miraculously fix those things. Suppose you don't know how to manage small responsibilities. In that case, you won't suddenly be equipped to handle much larger ones with little to no effort.

Relationships are mere reflections of who we all are within our core foundation and spirit. With that being said, could the struggle to find the right partner be an internal struggle with your identity?

For this book to work, you must do the work predicated on transparency, vulnerability, and accountability at the forefront.

Suppose you can vehemently and intentionally approach these concepts with an open mind and heart. In that case, you will kick down the doors and trample over hurdles that have long impeded your growth and alignment with yourself and others. If all is done successfully, you may finally realize and truly understand that the missing piece wasn't just finding 'Mr. Right'... it was finding 'You.'

Your unapologetically becoming the enhanced, more positive, healthier, and most amazing version of yourself will make you fall in love with life, your alignment, and your purpose and will attract and naturally lead you to the fulfilling relationship that awaits

Without a doubt, when you align internally, the proper connection follows most organically.

For you see, there's nothing you can do "wrong" to make the "right" person leave and nothing you can do "right" to make the "wrong" person stay.

The key is being honest about what you need and choosing wisely—because the man out there who is truly meant for you will recognize and value the best version of yourself.

CHAPTER 8

The '5' Men Every Woman Must Choose From

"The Motivated Hard Worker"

Men who grow up to become *motivated and hardworking* often share some common experiences from their childhood, even though each man's story is apparently different!

One thing many men do have in common is that they were raised by parents or caregivers who expected and required a lot from them—whether it was in school, sports, employment, familial responsibilities, or other areas of life. These parents usually supported, loved, and encouraged their male children. Still, they could also be too hard to please when things didn't go perfectly their way or as they expected from that male child. Thus, disappointing a loved one becomes a catastrophe that men, even at a young age, want to avoid at all costs!

Because of this, many young boys grow up sadly believing that they must *achieve something* to earn approval from others or to feel good about themselves! With this, the undue pressure to work harder and harder and to push themselves past newly enacted goalposts, past newer heights, and climb the proverbial mountains required of their loved ones.

A huge influence on young men at the impressionable times in their lives is the exposure to what they observed in their homes and the conspicuous examples inculcated into their daily lives.

As they grew in age and size, many driven men watched their parents throughout the years—especially their fathers or mothers—as they worked long hours or stayed committed to their familial and financial goals, even when life proved tough, and challenges were copious. Watching that kind of dedication taught the boy or young man that success takes time, focus, commitment, and incessant hard work.

A man's disposition and personality also play a considerable part in naturally becoming and being hardworking.

Some boys are naturally curious, enjoy learning how to solve problems, and enjoy education. When young boys try at something, subsequently succeed at that thing, and later get praised for it, they feel good *internally* about themselves and their achievement—and that pushes them to keep at it and keep going, to experience those pleasant and rewarding feelings again.

For other boys, their personal drive comes more from receiving *external*, tangible, palpable, or evidentiary rewards for their performances or achievements—like being admired, making money, or getting attention from loved ones, authority figures, or the opposite sex. Suppose that male grew up in a household where recognition and praise were a big deal and a direct or indirect result of their success or accolades. In that case, that need, or praise expectancy, could have become the young boy's primary motivator to prosper.

A male child's environment in which they grew up also mattered severely in his latter work disposition and responsibility makeup! If they had brothers or friends who were always competing with them—or trying to be the best or trying to get noticed—it can create the mindset that they too always needed to be "on top" or relentlessly strive to be!

In communities or cultures where success, money, and social status are highly valued, that pressure only increases. Along the way, teachers, coaches, or other role models who encouraged and required them to work hard to achieve great things might have inspired them, too.

Yet, let's be clear! It is not the case that every motivated, hardworking man came from a loving or supportive home. Many young boys grow up facing serious life challenges— things like poverty, unstable family and home life, abuse, neglect, displacement, abandonment, and other severe traumas. For these men, chasing success isn't just about merely being ambitious—it becomes a *way to survive*! Working hard gives these men with less-than-ordinary upbringings a sense of control, safety, and purpose in a world that may have once felt uncertain or unsafe. It becomes their way of coping, healing, belonging, existing, and proving to themselves and often others that they matter. It can rise above their past and circumstances!

Ironically, for some, these early life challenges and a young man's immense exposure to struggle can often lead to building powerful, invaluable qualities such as resilience, focus, and determination. Many of these men learn how to push through obstacles and stay committed to their goals no matter how hard things get. But with that strength often comes life struggles, curveballs, and the ensuing turmoil to overcome and triumph over.

For example, men who grew up tying their self-worth to their achievements often feel immense pressure to perform at their highest level. This can lead to perfectionism, a deep fear of failure, and a reluctance to take healthy risks or be emotionally vulnerable. In striving to meet unrealistic expectations, some push themselves to the brink of burnout.

From an early age, their sense of identity becomes deeply intertwined with doing, achieving, and excelling. As a result, it can feel nearly impossible to separate who they are from what they accomplish. Slowing down, resting, or asking for help can trigger feelings of inadequacy—as if they're falling behind or failing altogether.

In truth, a driven man is usually shaped by a mixture and combination of internal and external factors —such as his upbringing, the people he looked up to, his natural disposition and personality, and sometimes the relentlessly brutal childhood circumstances and environments in which he had to survive! All the above factors, just like the pieces of a puzzle ... all come together in the end to form the man he becomes and who people see standing there today.

Ultimately, knowing, understanding, and others being empathic to where his drive comes from helps us better understand both the *strengths* and the *struggles* behind the eyes and stance of every ambitious man we meet! These men may have proven to have impeccable and powerful work ethics, clear goals, and the deep desire to succeed—but these same men may also need just as much from others ... grace, understanding, and space to grow and evolve emotionally, especially within the context and safety of their relationships.

The 'Motivated Hard Worker' Core Traits

A driven and goal-oriented man usually has his sights set on success. He's highly focused and organized, whether climbing the corporate career ladder, building a business or enterprise, or chasing personal goals.

This kind of man thrives on routines, checks things off his to-do lists as he conquers each minuscule or significant feat, and explicitly sets clear plans for what he's doing and where he's going. This kind of man is confident and not cocky, well-spoken and outspoken, and often finds himself in leadership positions—because others naturally look to him to take charge.

Due to this, he often achieves financial stability and long-term success quite seamlessly and naturally.

In a relationship, his drive can be incredibly attractive to a woman, for he brings with him structure, purpose, and consistency! He knows what he wants and often inspires the woman to chase her dreams. Together, they can grow into a strong team—what many in society usually refer to as a "power couple." His ambition creates an atmosphere where setting goals, leveling up, and dreaming bigger becomes a shared journey with this lady in mind and by his side.

Yet, there's a slight caveat because with all that passion and focus comes a few challenges that his partner will have to inevitably and ultimately endure when going on this relationship journey with him.

You see, sometimes this kind of man, his dedication to those goals, and his commitment to work can take over both his work and personal life! He might become so wrapped up in his goals that he forgets to slow down and spend time with those he loves and those who similarly love and cherish him. He may expect the same level of drive from his partner when in a relationship— and if she has a different pace or style, this can create tension or sometimes unintentional resentment.

Without realizing it, he might start treating the relationship like another item on his to-do list, missing out on the emotional connection that love truly affords him and usually requires of him!

Thus, the key for this type of man is learning that relationships aren't about perfection or performance—they're about inimitable presence. They need time to vest in, quality time to cultivate and nourish the soil of the relationship, care to express the love between the two people in the relationship, and accountability, sincerity, and vulnerability, just like any meaningful goal in life.

For the type of woman dating this type of man, it's important to admire his ambition and *remind him that love is not a race to win—it's a place to call home, rest, grow, and ... belong!*

"The Passionate Dreamer"

Men who grow up to be 'Passionate Dreamers' often carry something special within them—a deep innate belief in the importance of love, emotional connections, and the hope of finding that one perfect someone. This isn't something these men wake up feeling or believing one day. These convictions and ideologies existed and started in childhood, shaped by how they were raised, nurtured, trained, mentored, and experienced love early on!

One of the most significant influences for this kind of man is how they were emotionally connected to their parents, guardians, or caregivers in their youth. If a young boy grew up in a home where love was steady and constant—where hugs, kind words, and emotional support were normalized—he likely developed a secure sense of what love should feel like and how it should be received and expressed. These types of men often grow into adults who are hopeful about love. They believe that deep, lasting relationships are possible because that's what they were shown from early adolescence.

On the other hand, if a boy grew up in a home where love was inconsistent or nonexistent—where the emotions and expression of love from parents, guardians, or caregivers, one minute was hot, and the next instant was cold—he may have learned that affection wasn't and still isn't always a safe or reliable bet.

As a result, the same boy may grow into a man who craves deep devotion and constantly seeks reassurance in relationships. It's not that he is needy—in fact, he may be innocently and instinctively just trying to find the emotional stability he missed out on as a child with his partner in his current relationship. Thus, this type of man may idealize love, searching for a partner to give him the safety and emotional closeness he's always longed for.

Family dynamics most emphatically have also shaped how a man views romance. If his parents or guardians openly showed love to one another—through affection, teamwork, and support—he may grow up expecting relationships to be full of tenderness and deep connection. But if his home was filled with tension, distance, or emotional coldness, he might cope by dreaming of a love that's the opposite of what he saw growing up. His idealism courageously and commendably becomes a kind of emotional hope—a vision of what love *could* be, even if he never saw it firsthand as a child.

Some boys grow up with *naturally sensitive and empathetic hearts*. These children often deeply feel emotions and are quick to care about others empathically. Because of this, they may find themselves drawn to stories of chivalry, knights rescuing maidens, heroic-themed fairy tales, romance stories where the guy courts and wins the girl, or even daydreams about a "happily ever after" with the one.

Love isn't just a feeling for them—it becomes something supernatural and almost divine. It becomes something big, something that sweeps you off your feet. Over time, these boys may grow into men who believe love should always feel deep, intense, and extraordinary.

Validation also plays a role in shaping these beliefs. A boy praised for being kind, sweet, or emotionally expressive may grow up thinking that *big romantic gestures* are the way to show love. Suppose he's constantly told he's a "good boy" for being thoughtful or gentle. In that case, he may begin to believe that being deeply romantic makes him valuable in a relationship. On the flip side, if his emotional needs were ignored or dismissed as a child, he might escape into fantasies about the perfect love— imagining someone who will finally see him, accept him, and reciprocally love him completely.

Cultural influences only make these ideas stronger. From movies to music to books, the message is often the same: real love is dramatic, intense, and meant to feel like destiny is actualized. When a young boy, in all his impressionable glory, keeps hearing and seeing these continuous messages in the media and entertainment he absorbs, he may start believing that anything less than *epic love* isn't real love. He begins to expect fireworks, the reuniting and finding of soulmates, and moments that feel like they came straight out of a movie scene.

As he grows older, this type of man—what we might call a Passionate Dreamer—brings a lot of hope and heart into his relationship with his significant other. He wants to love deeply. He wants to feel emotionally connected. And when things align with his romantic ideals, he can be incredibly joyful, generous, and devoted.

Yet, real-life relationships aren't always perfect. Just the opposite! Life isn't a movie scene, and relationships are subjective to the two people experiencing it together. Real-life relationships are messy, unpredictable, and full of learning moments. So, usually when reality doesn't match the dream of the 'Passionate Dreamer,' this kind of man can feel wholly disappointed, or even genuinely heartbroken—not because his partner failed him, but because his inner story about how love "should be" didn't play out the way he imagined or hoped for.

This is why it's so crucial for Passionate Dreamers to reflect on their childhood days and memories and explore where their notions and ideas about love came from. Understanding how their childhood, upbringing, movies, reality shows, music, and pop culture shaped their romantic hopes can help them *balance their dreams with reality*.

True love may not always feel like a fairytale. Still, true love can prove to be *honest, beautiful, and lasting* when both partners are willing to grow through imperfections.

The 'Passionate Dreamer' Core Traits

The 'passionate dreamer' is profoundly emotional and openly affectionate. He wears his heart on his sleeve; he's never shy about sharing his feelings. He shows love in deeply personal ways, whether through sweet compliments, thoughtful gifts, or little surprises—like a handwritten note or flowers for no reason. He's the kind of man who's drawn to beauty and meaning. He may love art, poetry, music, or get lost in his thoughts. In his heart, he believes in soulmates, fairy-tale love, and happily-ever-afters.

He wants a deep and authentic connection when he's in a relationship. He doesn't hold back when showing how much he cares. He might be the guy who plans a romantic dinner just because or leaves a kind message for you to find in the morning. He listens well, often intuitively picking up on emotions that others may miss, and truly tries to understand his partner's heart. Being around him can feel warm, tender, and emotionally rich.

Yet, because he's such a romantic and a dreamer, he sometimes may struggle with the more practical tasks of life, such as paying bills on time or keeping up with chores at home.

Managing daily responsibilities might feel boring, burdensome, or overwhelming. He lives for moments of passion and excitement and sometimes wants to avoid the routine stuff of life because he feels it kills his spark.

Another challenge for the 'passionate dreamer' is that he may expect too much from a relationship. In his mind, relationships are supposed to feel supposedly magical all the time. So, when everyday problems appear—as they do in all relationships—the 'passionate dreamer might interpret this devastatingly and feel disheartened. Suppose his partner doesn't conform to the picture he has idealized and has painted in his mind. In that case, disappointment can unrealistically settle in quickly. It's not necessarily that he doesn't love her—it's just that reality didn't match the story he conjured up in his mind over the years and was ultimately holding on to!

In the end, when this kind of man learns that relationships aren't all necessarily poetic and involve grassy knolls, white horses, and damsels in distress. Instead, he will discover that love *is* a real emotion, experience, and verb worth nurturing even through the challenging and monotonous days—and then and only then, he can become a truly amazing, engaging, and reliable partner for the remarkable woman in his life.

His depth, affection, and emotional openness will then be able to healthily procure a sense of wonder and emotional safety in his relationship. The ongoing key is to help him stay grounded while still allowing space for him to thrive and dream passionately.

3

"The Dependable – Peacekeeper"

Men who eventually become Dependable Peacekeepers are known for being steady, dependable, and calm—even during stressful and challenging times. These men are simply the type of men that you can count on, who are inherently keen on keeping everything running smoothly. Nevertheless, many people don't see or know that his qualities are often shaped by the experiences they have endured when growing up. In many instances, these men were forced to grow up rather quickly. Maybe one parent wasn't around, or the family went through financial struggles or experienced the long-term illnesses of a loved one.

As young boys, they may have stepped up and stepped in to help care for their loved ones or a close relative—thus undertaking responsibilities far beyond what kids their age should've had to handle or endure. Over time, these young 'dependable' boys learned that being in control, hiding emotions, and holding it all together ... seemed to make everyone feel safer and not have to worry about him. That pressure to always be "the strong one" became part of who they are, even today!

In other situations, these men were raised in families where emotions weren't openly shared. Maybe they were told things like "Big boys don't cry" or "Be tough." even when those words weren't spoken directly, they often got the message that showing emotions was seen as their being considered weak by the adult figures or older males around them.

Eventually, these young boys quickly learned to hide their true feelings or any semblance of emotions. They taught them to deal with their problems quietly! This helped them become self-reliant but also made it hard to open up to others or ask for the simplest kind of help or assistance from anyone—even when they truly need it!

Some of these men grew up in homes full of conflict or chaos, where arguments were common, and the home atmosphere was highly unpredictable and terrifyingly tense!

In those situations, these young boys often became the inexperienced peacekeepers for the adults in those environments—and were thus charged or looked to be the ones who calmed everyone down and kept the peace when things became tumultuous. These men successfully learned to read the room, stay calm under immense pressure, and learn how to make others feel safe in an environment, even when they didn't feel safe or protected themselves.

While these young boys became great at keeping everyone else stable, they often started to believe their own feelings didn't matter as much. Their role became "the rock"—always steady and strong.

Sometimes, growing up in a home where life constantly felt uncertain made those young boys grow up into men who craved and required being in control. Being dependable gave them a sense of security and, often at times, purpose. As adults, this shows up in how they plan carefully, handle responsibilities, and do everything consistently. Society usually praises these qualities, so they lean into them even more.

These men make truly amazing partners. They're loyal, naturally calm, empathically thoughtful, and deeply committed in relationships. Yet, it is important to mention that these men also carry emotional weight that others don't always see. They are used to being the strong ones, so they usually struggle to admit when they're hurting, wrong, afraid, or overwhelmed. They rarely ask for help, or to be honest ... they may not even know how to. They usually feel unappreciated or feel that they are advantageously and constantly being taken for granted. Because of this, quiet resentment can build up internally over time!

The key to a "Dependable Peacekeeper" is learning that it is okay to be vulnerable as a man in control of his emotions and purpose. Expressing emotions doesn't make him weak—it makes him human. When he allows himself to rest, be cared for, or say, "I'm not okay," he creates space for a more balanced life and a healthier relationship. After all, being strong doesn't mean carrying the whole world on one's back alone—when you meet the 'one' ... it means knowing you no longer have to!

The 'Dependable Peacekeeper' Core Traits

Men deemed dependable and loyal often become the steadfast, reliable presence in their families and friendships. They're the ones who keep their word, show up when they say they will, and make others feel safe simply because of their constant and consistent nature.

These men don't usually chase after excitement; they don't tend to thrill-seek or value sporadic or abrupt change. Instead, these men feel most at peace when their lives are very organized and predictable. Routines give them a sense of control, and they often prefer calm, steady days over surprises and frivolous spontaneity.

Because of this, they're known for being very patient, kind, and emotionally steady. When life gets overwhelming, they're the kind of person people run to for comfort and level-headed advice. They offer emotional security and a sense of peace just from their presence and just from their words.

These men often bring a strong commitment and understanding of family values in relationships. They think only in the long term. They're known for making plans for the future, and they work hard to make sure their loved ones are perpetually cared for. You can count on them in good times and when things get rough. Their loyalty isn't something that needs to be questioned—it's characteristically part of who they are.

However, there are moments when their love for structure can become quite a challenge. Their need for stability can make them hesitant about change, even if it can lead to good change. Taking risks—moving to a new place, switching careers, or trying something bold—can feel overwhelming for them. To others, because they cling so tightly to their routine, they might come across as boring.

Yet, where they seemingly lack spontaneity, they entirely make up for devotion and trustworthiness. Although their consistent personality may not always make a woman's heart race or flutter, the same consistency will bring peace to a woman's soul.

Essentially, the "dependable peacekeeper" will offer a safe place to land when life feels uncertain and a kind of love built to last a lifetime.

"The Thrill-Seeker"

The "Thrill-Seeker" type of man is full of an exorbitant amount of energy. Because of this, he is always looking for adventure and rarely sits still for long. Whether he's into skydiving, spontaneous road trips, or trying something new just for the experience or the 'thrill' of things, his personality is wired for his incessant search for excitement. Yet, this kind of personality did not appear overnight. This free-spirited-natured personality often took shape very early in life.

Many men who grew into adventurous adults grew up in homes where curiosity and exploration were encouraged as young boys. Maybe their families went on many camping trips, traveled often together, or allowed them to play outside or try new creative things. When parents, guardians, or caregivers praised them for being brave, trying something new, or stepping outside their comfort zone, they learned early on that discovery and risk could be not only *fun* but also fulfilling and *rewarding*. Essentially, the positive reinforcement they received made adventures feel like a good thing and ultimately desirable.

Some also had families that allowed them to make their own choices. Whether it was picking their own choice of hobbies, deciding how to spend their time, or even choosing what they wanted to explore, this freedom helped them build confidence. They started believing they could handle whatever came their way and carried that boldness into adulthood.

It's also true that some people are just naturally drawn to excitement. Even as children, they may have craved newness, spontaneity, action, adventures, and stimulation. If that part of their personality was supported—and not shut down as children—they grew up embracing that side of themselves. Whether being outgoing and loud or quieter and observant, their desire for new experiences shows how they live and express their love today.

So, while not every 'Thrill-Seeker' had the same kind of childhood, many were often encouraged to be bold, innovative, given the necessary room to grow, and naturally inclined to chase the thrill of ... well, the unknown!

Young boys who are emotionally intense and can easily bounce back from setbacks are often more open to trying new things later in life! They don't allow small failures to keep them down for long, and this helps them grow into confident, adventurous adults. When parents teach healthy ways to overcome the mundane and for their kids to take more significant risks—by encouraging their children's intrinsic curiosity and by not punishing them for their mistakes—those kids essentially learn that it's okay to step into the unknown. Over time, and when they enter adulthood, they develop a sense of control in life and experience less fear when facing new or challenging situations.

The priceless values thus taught and obtained at home or within a child's cultural environment, in the end, will make a world of difference. Kids are often fortified to follow their paths in families or communities where independence and self-discovery are encouraged and celebrated. The child hears stories about courageous ancestors, watches movies and television shows, reads books about explorers, and observes adults being brave in challenging circumstances; together, they can leave a lasting impression on him. The kid grows up thinking, "An adventurer is who I am." Thus, incorporating this adventurer persona no longer feels like a mere choice for him—but feels like a part of his core and actual identity.

Yet, to be realistic, not every free-spirited person came from a supportive and loving background. Sometimes, their love for freedom and new experiences grew from the *opposite*—from their feeling trapped or controlled as a child!

Suppose a young boy grew up in a strict home where his choices were limited and his opinions didn't matter. In that case, he might consequently develop a strong desire to break free as an adult. For others, painful childhood experiences—like family conflict, trauma, abuse, neglect, abandonment, rejection, or instability—can make them feel displaced, restless, and unexplainably agitated when alone or even when around others. Sometimes, they are constantly moving and always chasing something new. They might be trying to outrun the emotional weight of their past, which felt painful, smothering, or stagnating.

In these cases, being adventurous isn't just about exploring the world—it's also about searching for healing, freedom, and peace within. Sometimes, it can be healthy and empowering. Other times, it's just a way to avoid facing unresolved emotions.

When these men reach their teens, many show strong signs of being free-spirited. Whether it's through traveling, sports, music, or trying different friend groups, they often push against expectations and what is deemed conventional. They want to find what suits them—not what has been chosen for them.

As these adventurous young men grow up, so does their sense of independence. Many take on part-time jobs, start small businesses, or throw themselves into creative projects. They want to test how far they can go alone—without feeling like they are being boxed in. This gnawing need for freedom and exploration becomes the foundation for living their lives as adults!

When these men enter adulthood, their "Thrill-Seeker" personality often appears differently. You might see it in their constant job changes, their choice of a non-traditional career path, or their incessant love for traveling and spontaneous experiences. They usually have a deep curiosity about life and always learn something new. They're often seen as "lifelong learners." They are always excited about discovering what is waiting for them around the next corner.

While this kind of openness can lead to tremendous personal growth and unforgettable life experiences, it can also make it harder for them to settle down with a partner. These men may resist long-term commitments like marriage, home buying, or following a typical career path. It's not that they don't value those things—it's just that such a heightened semblance of stability and commitment can make them feel there will now be limitations on their freedom and autonomy.

Over time, many learn how to find some healthy balance—to keep their adventurous spirit alive while building stable relationships, careers, and promising futures. It thus becomes a personal journey of learning how to satisfy both their innate need for freedom and their emotional needs from the people they love, who, in return, love them back.

The truth is that a man with an innate thrill-seeking nature often results from a mix of influences. Maybe his curiosity was encouraged early on, or he may have been born with a natural desire for excitement. In some cases, that need for freedom comes from growing up in a controlling, painful, or traumatic environment. Whatever the path taken or the journeys sojourned, these experiences have helped to shape his deep drive to explore, take risks, and live life on his terms.

It is similarly important to understand that not every kind of adventure should be deemed a healthy one! A true free spirit knows how to balance freedom with responsibility. He understands the value of boundaries, emotional maturity, and his choices' impact on those around him. When he learns that, his adventurous heart becomes not just exciting—but deeply grounded and inspiring to others as well.

The 'Thrill Seeker' Core Traits

He is a man who is spontaneous and full of curiosity. His life is an open road—ready to be explored at every turn! Whether by trying out new foods, going on a last-minute trip, or starting an unexpected hobby, he *lives for the moment*. He doesn't like feeling boxed in by rules or routines, and he usually chooses his own path—even if it's not the most traditional one. His free-spirited nature makes him energetic, playful, and full of surprises. With him around, even the most ordinary day can suddenly become an adventure.

This type of man brings a refreshing sense of fun and excitement to a relationship. He encourages his partner to try new things, take chances, and release fear. You might find yourself doing things you never imagined—visiting new places together, trying out unusual activities or trying new food, and even rethinking what your "comfort zone" truly means. He genuinely believes that the best way to grow is by continuing to stretch beyond the familiar. With this notion... he loves to bring the woman he loves ... undoubtedly, for an unforgettable ride.

Yet, regardless of all that fire, passion, innovation, and freedom, there are also some real challenges to discuss. For instance, this type of male's constant need for stimulation can make life with him feel somewhat unpredictable—especially for a woman who craves calm, order, or long-term planning. Unfortunately, when he feels and believes committing to her might limit his freedom, he may pull away or hesitate to settle down. It's not necessarily that the 'thrill-seeker' doesn't care—it's just that the idea of "forever" can feel like a cage, prison, or coffin...for someone who values fluidity, movement, change, and unpredictability!

Sometimes, he can also be impulsive and imprudent, making hasty decisions without considering the resulting impact or irrevocable consequences. Unfortunately, Such consequences might appear in their finances, sudden changes and abrupt planning, or in their emotional reactions to things or others, which can feel intense one minute and gone the next! Ironically, the thrill-seeker's heart is in the right place. Still, suppose he doesn't learn to balance his adventurous spirit with his responsible side. In that case, he can consequently strain his relationship negatively.

For the remarkable woman in his life, balance is the key to loving this kind of man—and for him to love back in return.

When the 'thrill-seeker' learns how to ground his free spirit without losing it, he brings passion and depth to a relationship. As a result, with the right partner, that fusion of adventure and emotional growth can create a one-of-a-kind, beautiful connection.

5

"The Intellect Philosopher"

The term "Intellect Philosopher" or the "intellectual philosopher" isn't something you'll find anywhere in psychology textbooks. This term helps to describe a specific kind of man—a deep thinker who values ideas, meaningful conversations, culture, and mental stimulation in his relationships. These men light up when discussing big topics like history, philosophy, science, or current events. They're thoughtful, curious, and love getting lost in a good book or an inspiring conversation!

This kind of male mindset often takes root early in life. As young boys, many of these men were praised for being smart—for using big words, solving problems quickly, or doing well in school. Over time, they started to believe that their intelligence was the most valuable part of who they were. Suppose they grew up in families that 'didn't' encourage open emotional expression. In that case, they may have learned that thinking and logic were "safe zones" of them. At the same time, sharing feelings was way too risky, unnecessary, or uncomfortable.

Some men had intellectual role models at home—parents, guardians, or caregivers who encouraged learning, reading, or academic success. In other cases, if home life was chaotic or emotionally distant, books and ideas began to form a means of escape. When emotions were just too much to handle, their turning to knowledge allowed them to feel a sense of control and peace!

Socially, growing up wasn't always easy for the intellectual philosopher. They may have felt slightly different from their peers, especially if they were more introverted. While other kids were out socializing, they were often happier reading or thinking. Sometimes, they felt admired for their brains but felt left out regarding more casual or emotional connections.

As these men got older, their identity often became tied to being "the smart one"—the person people turn to for answers, advice, guidance, tutoring, or thoughtful insight. Although this can be a beautiful gift, it can also come with a cost! One of sheer loneliness, or not always feeling comfortable around others to be vulnerable or feel okay to open up emotionally, as they were trained relentlessly that it was more important to value intellect over emotions!

For men who grew into "Intellect Philosophers," early life experiences often shaped how they dealt with the array of their emotions—especially the difficult ones. Instead of these men being able to sit with their feelings or talk them out, they learned to keep everything inside. They learned to unfortunately handle their pain and stress without turning to others. Sadly, this measure of solitude only confused them because they had to think their way through things *alone*.

As kids, they may have discovered that analyzing a problem gave them a better sense of control, especially if their home life was less than ideal, unpredictable, traumatic, or emotionally distant. Over time, such dedication and their exceptional problem-solving skills became a coping mechanism for them—where logic replaced emotions, and getting lost in their throngs of books, puzzles, knowledge, and information for them became a safe haven of sorts!

As adults, these men are often considered deep thinkers who love sharing their ideas and acquired philosophy. They're naturally drawn to women who can keep up with them intellectually—similarly, someone who enjoys meaningful conversations about life, the world, and everything in between.

For this type of mind, intimacy begins with the mind! Whether such intimacy involves talking about a great book, an ethical dilemma, or even the news, it all can feel as romantic to them as a candlelit dinner!

Yet, here's where it can get tricky! When deeper emotional needs come up—like when a woman wants to feel *understood* by him and not just *heard*—the 'Intellect Philosopher' might struggle a bit with this task. He may not even realize that he's avoiding emotion by analyzing it. He could genuinely care deeply about the woman. Still, he might come across as distant when trying to show love in his way, especially if he does so by leading with facts instead of his feelings.

With the 'intellect philosopher,' another pattern that shows up in his relationships is that he can sometimes slip into "teacher or professor mode." He may just want to kindly offer some advice or want to explain something specific to someone in greater detail—which is something that inherently feels natural to him but may come across as condescending if his partner was looking for empathy and a shoulder to lean on and not looking for a lesson, lecture or a solution to what she only wanted to vent to you about.

Although the advice the 'intellect philosopher' tries to share with his loved one generously is rarely meant to hurt her, if unsolicited and if not well-balanced with his ability to be able to listen to her or be that emotional presence she desires, it can cause continuous frustration and resentment within her!

However, it is important to remember that not all Intellect Philosophers come from the same background. As mentioned, some grew up in exceptionally warm and loving families that valued learning, knowledge, and open conversations. Others emphatically turned their attention and focused on books and learning to survive the emotional void or distance in their childhood environments and any familial struggles they experienced.

No two stories are ever precisely the same, but the common thread is that these men grew up feeling seen and valued for their minds, if for nothing else! So naturally, they believe that sharing their intellectual thoughts, insights, and ideas is the deepest and most genuine way to connect with a woman naturally.

When they are loved well by a woman—and when they learn to fuse the use of their heart with their mind—Intellect Philosophers can be extremely loyal, thoughtful, and deeply attentive partners. However, they must equally remember that emotional connections need to be learned and practiced, no different than any skill they have acquired and intellectually mastered over the years. When these types of men begin to trust the emotional side of their lives as much as the logical and prudent side, the real essence of the relationships they find themselves in will finally come to life and come to fruition!

The 'Intellect Philosopher' Core Traits

Men who rightfully fall into the "Intellect Philosopher" category are avid deep thinkers with curious spirits. They're the ones who are always watching documentaries, reading books, or diving into meaningful conversations. These men don't just accept things at face value—they want to understand *why* something is valued as such! Their minds are constantly turning and going, and they're quick to pick up on and catch small details or inconsistencies in conversations that others might miss!

They often prefer quiet or one-on-one settings over big crowds. Large social gatherings can feel draining or overwhelming, yet if they sit them down for a thoughtful talk with someone they trust, you can see them come alive!

In relationships, this preference for depth means they value authentic connections. These men want to *know* the woman they are with—not just the surface or superficial stuff, but the heart and true essence of who she is, her thoughts, and her dreams. This makes them perfect for meaningful conversations and discussions, demonstrating mutual respect and growing closer together.

These men are intrinsically great problem-solvers. Instead of responding to conflict emotionally, they tend to stay stoically calm and look at situations quite logically. They think carefully, weigh all the pros and cons, and offer grounded solutions. When their partner has ambitions or goals, they're usually very supportive. They love encouraging people that they care about and love to genuinely support them in their quest to grow, learn, and become the best version of themselves!

However, just like anyone else, these men come with their own set of challenges. Because they spend so much time with themselves in their heads, they can sometimes miss out on what's happening emotionally—both within their selves and within others. They may love profoundly and heartfully but have trouble expressing it in ways that will be interpreted as romantic, warm, or emotionally invoking. If they don't take care, they can also come across as distant, unfeeling, heartless, and cold, even though that's not their intention and the furthest from how they truly feel.

These men often struggle with overthinking and overanalyzing everything! Instead of simply enjoying the moment or environments they find themselves in, they sometimes can't help but analyze every detail or try to predict every possible outcome. While this can make them seem wise and thoughtful in some circumstances, in other circumstances, it just seems like it's hard for them to relax and enjoy the sweet rewards and nectar to be found in a relationship.

The good news is that when a woman understands his unusual yet unique nature, in conjunction with her genuine patience for his ways, he ultimately can learn how to open up emotionally. Due to this, the Intellect Philosopher is mainly found to be a deeply committed and enriching partner in a relationship who is loyal and loving. This type of man brings love to the relationship and wisdom, growth, and emotional depth to the table!

Because the 'Intellect Philosopher' relies so much on logic and reasoning, they can sometimes make their partner feel unheard—especially when their emotions are involved. If a woman shares her feelings with him, and he responds with facts or analyses, it might feel to her like he's brushing her off or missing the point entirely! He doesn't necessarily mean to do this, which may not be his intentional goal during their deep discussions. It's probable that since childhood, his instinct has been to fix situations and solve problems using logic rather than a brunt emotion! All these things can unintentionally distance the woman from the 'intellect philosopher.'

Unfortunately, when he genuinely tries to make sense of things intellectually, it might feel to his partner that he's blatantly ignoring how she feels. That's why learning to balance deep thinking and being emotionally present is crucial for him and the sustainability of his relationship. When he takes the time to understand things and *feel things with* his partner, something powerful happens: the relationship becomes more mentally and emotionally fulfilling, and intimacy prevails.

If done right, when a remarkable woman loves an intellect philosopher, it can feel like she is being with someone who stimulates their mind and respects their heart—a truly rare and beautiful combination.

Chapter 9

Compatibility Pairing

Now that we've learned about the '5' types of Men That Every Women Has to Choose from, we will look next to the concept, science, and art behind compatibility pairing in this chapter.

The idea behind the '5' Types of Men comes from the belief that every man's personality and relationship style is shaped by his life experiences, upbringing, and personal growth. While most men deeply desire respect, admiration, and intimacy, they show it differently. Their actions in relationships often reflect the values they were taught, the emotional experiences they've had, and how much they've grown over time.

This is why women must do their own inner work first—to heal from past hurts, understand their emotional patterns, and get clear on what they truly want in a relationship. When a woman knows herself deeply, she can more easily recognize which of the 'five' types of men best aligns with her values, emotional needs, and long-term desires.

It's not just about choosing the "right man"—it's about being the "right woman" for the kind of love and partnership you genuinely want.

Understanding the Male Ego and Emotional Responses

Men, by nature, thrive on feeling valued and respected in relationships. A woman's perception of him is crucial in shaping his confidence. If she compares him to another man in a way that implies he is lacking or inadequate, it can profoundly affect his self-worth.

Even if the man struggles with assertiveness, leadership, or decision-making, feeling inferior can cause him to withdraw emotionally from the relationship.

Respect is a driving force in a man's emotional commitment. When a woman reassures him of his valuation and worth and acknowledges his efforts, he is likelier to remain engaged and committed. On the other hand, if he constantly feels undermined or unappreciated, he may seek validation elsewhere or hesitate to invest fully in the relationship.

What Angers Men

Men, in theory, are self-aware beings. They are told the truth about themselves from childhood. For example, their fathers toughen them up as they get older. Statements like, you are now in charge whenever the father leaves home for work or doing the heavy lifting in their homes, such as taking the trash out, cutting the lawn, or working on a farm, toughens them up. They must deal with the realities of the external environment and, most importantly, learn how to protect their families from a young age. Even when physically challenged, they'll find ways to accomplish these tasks. Whenever they fall short, corrections are made in a straightforward manner. So, men are self-aware, and their strengths and weaknesses are publicly displayed.

Men are trained and learn not to show emotions at a young age, mostly from male family members and close friends. They know how to fight and play sports and are highly competitive.

What angers men is when they finally find the 'one.' That woman they have been looking for all their lives, and unfortunately, as life would have it, she has experienced pain and suffering before even meeting him.

Men will not easily show emotionally that they are angry at the tough life she has been through. And this is because they were not there to protect her, even if not retrospectively possible or a feasible option for him! Yet, that feeling of powerlessness is sometimes disastrously projected onto his relationship and interpreted to the woman to feel acts of his emotional detachment.

Men are very territorial by nature, and so women need to understand that as fixers and boundary keepers, men take it to heart when they see the pain and suffering their women have gone through before meeting them, especially if she has been in a relationship before meeting them, that caused her pain or harm, either resulting in physical or her emotional scars.

Additionally, men are hurt by past rejections from women. This may sound unfamiliar to some, but it happens more often.

Women normally accept intimacy from men whom they find attractive. But the men they reject are emotionally hurt even though they appear tough on the outside. Remember, men are generally trained not to show emotions, but the pain is there. So, most men have encountered a woman who rejects sex or physical intimacy but would prefer to keep them as friends. When women do this, those men are trapped in the friend zone, and since they do not know how to get out of it, they go far and beyond what the "bad boy" does in an attempt to woe them.

As expected, this never works. So, that baggage is buried in their subconscious. So, they may seek a relationship with a woman they see as less attractive or desperate for attention and love.

This is where men who suffer from low esteem finally get an opportunity to date and experience both physical and emotional intimacy. The aftermath involves the same woman giving them a chance because of the hurt they've experienced from rejection.

Now, another group of men are the 'people pleasers.' They find themselves over-giving to women who have earned the right to do so. For example, they may treat a date like a spouse instead of affording her the space to earn that level of treatment. So when women sense that they are getting more than what they deserve, even though they appreciate or, in some cases, take advantage of a lovely man's generosity, their conscience is riddled with guilt. Eventually, they end up breaking up with the 'nice guy' out ... of pity.

I might also add that when women meet a man they see as marriage material or a keeper, they also tend to withhold physical intimacy or sex to prove their chastity or their worth. This also hurts men, especially if the woman is not a virgin or has been intimate before. Now, it doesn't mean that the woman does not have the right not to be intimate. It means that men are confused about understanding why physical intimacy or sex is being withheld after meeting them.

This makes men question if they are good enough compared to the past lovers she chose to sleep with or have sex with. In many cases, the inadvertently discouraged men will seek physical intimacy elsewhere. This is also a layer of anger and frustration that men harbor on the inside from this sort of shame that the woman unknowingly casts on him.

In social media circles, the term commonly used is "red pill," meaning that men choose to go their own way. They quit dating and relationships altogether.

I know women have questions about how men can choose to go without physical intimacy when it's generally assumed that sex is all that men think about. But, contrary to popular belief, men can learn how to control their sex drives and their desires.

Just like in sports, some athletes will stay away from sex and other forms of physical intimacy to enhance their performance and concentration levels. They do this because these types of men have chosen to embark on their lives of achieving their goals and thus creating wealth for future generations rather than wasting time seeking fruitless relationships with women.

Although it seems harsh, it's important to mention that once some of these men succeed, the unresolved anger from the women who rejected them in the past, unfortunately, follows them throughout life and their success.

Hence, the popular phrase 'gold digger' comes into play when these men begin to interact with women in the later stages of life. These successful men are likely to believe that once successful, women want their wealth after being rejected before.

A famous rapper once said that while struggling to get on his feet, he would frequent a certain club, a venue known for hip-hop artists. Now, while there, he took note of an attractive woman. He went after her with all he had, but she would not go out with him. His heart was broken, but as expected in the music industry and being a man, he had to shield his emotions. Fast forward, as fate would have it, he rose to fame and became a legendary artist in his own right.

During one of his visits to give back to the community, and after the event, he decided to visit the same club. Upon arrival, his fans went wild; the press and everyone who knew him in the music and entertainment world were in attendance. Also in attendance was the attractive woman he attempted to date recently. He watched her enter the crowd in tears of excitement, hugging him and telling him that she loves him and has never stopped doing so since the first time they met.

The artist was aghast and in shock at the blatant change of tune she was now having. Having seen so many people experiencing so much fame, he shook his head because it seemed that someone claimed to know him everywhere he went.

It was confusing and bittersweet to separate who was telling the truth and who cared about him. But this woman was no other woman. It would be impossible to feign a connection with her or find any genuineness in her statement. He knew he remembered who she was. He recalled that experience of being rejected by her as if it was only yesterday. In his mind, her memory was sealed and selective.

Seeing her beauty and watching her falling apart created empathy for her and a form of relational regret for him. While he felt something in him for her, he was also caught in a cognitive dissonance. How could she say she loved him and rejected him? How could she be those two very different things to him simultaneously?

Regardless of his trying, he simply could not reconcile the two sides of this coin.

He furiously told her, "When I wanted you, I was a nobody but a young man with a dream. I needed you, wanted you to be mine. But you chose another path." The reality is that he was mad because he could not understand how the same woman who rejected him now wanted him.

Most men experience the same effect with their ex-lovers. When they return to them, these men experience painful and very conflicting emotions. On the one hand, they had to master the courage to ask these women out. On the other hand, they were not good enough for whatever underlying or trivial reason, which led the women to break up with them. So, when ex-lovers return, men are somewhat irritated, slightly bitter, and can even project this anger and slight from these past experiences with certain kinds of women onto their new and unsuspecting female lovers.

That is what men need to address as emotional baggage.

Beyond Labels: Examining Male Identity

Terms like alpha, beta, and sigma males have been popularized as a way to categorize masculinity. Still, these labels do not fully define a man's character or relationship potential. While the alpha male is often seen as dominant and assertive, success in relationships isn't solely determined by dominance— it also requires emotional intelligence, empathy, and stability.

Men who hold positions of power, wealth, or influence may appear to have everything. Yet, many struggle with relationship challenges, trust issues, and emotional isolation. High-status individuals often face intense scrutiny, financial risks, and personal betrayals, proving that material success does not always equate to relational happiness.

The Reality of Status and Power in Relationships

Many men work hard to achieve financial stability or career success, believing it will attract the right partner and create a fulfilling life. However, success also comes with challenges—increased expectations, external pressures, and sometimes difficulty forming genuine connections.

Women seeking long-term relationships should focus on more than a man's status or achievements. Instead, they should consider his values, emotional depth, and relationship consistency.

Key Questions to Ask When Evaluating a Partner

Instead of relying on broad categories or assumptions, women should observe a man's behavior over time:

- Does he communicate openly and listen to your needs?

- How does he handle conflict and setbacks?

- Is he emotionally available and willing to invest in the relationship?

- Does he align with your long-term values and priorities?

By shifting the focus from labels and stereotypes to core values and compatibility, women can make more informed relationship choices, ensuring they choose a partner who is not only prosperous on the outside but also emotionally stable, committed, and capable of genuine connection.

Many women face challenges finding a compatible partner because cultural and social programming often teaches them to prioritize certain superficial or stereotypical traits—such as height, weight, or traditional notions of "money and success."

These factors are primarily phenotypic, meaning they stem from physical appearance or other observable characteristics that can change with time.

Indeed, we can all agree that looks and other surface-level attributes rarely remain constant throughout the span of a relationship. By women seeking to focus too heavily on these short-term markers—like preferring a partner to be above a specific height or fit a certain physical mold—women may overlook deeper, more enduring qualities that foster long-term compatibility.

Emotional intelligence, shared values, similar life goals, and genuine interpersonal chemistry are all far more critical to sustaining a fulfilling partnership over the years. Unfortunately, many people miss out on potentially excellent matches because their internal or societal stereotypes and ingrained beliefs keep them from exploring connections with someone who doesn't meet these arbitrary criteria.

Moreover, relying on external traits can lead to relationship difficulties down the road. When beauty fades, or body shapes shift—which inevitably happens—couples who base their bond primarily on physical attraction may struggle to maintain closeness. In contrast, couples building connections on intellectual synergy, emotional support, shared purpose, or complementary personalities have a more stable foundation. As life circumstances evolve, these partnerships adapt because they aren't anchored solely in surface-level qualities.

Ultimately, recognizing the Intellect Philosopher's value of long-term compatibility over short-term phenotypic appeal to the Intellect Philosopher can help women (and men) approach dating and relationships more intentionally.

This means asking more profound questions about someone's character, life vision, emotional readiness, and relational habits. When people look beyond stereotypes—be they related to appearance, status, or arbitrary social "rules"—they open themselves up to richer, more sustainable partnerships that truly complement who they are and who they aspire to become. These are storytelling tools or starting points for creating compelling relationship dynamics.

Real people are more nuanced than simple labels, of course. Still, archetypes can serve as a helpful framework for highlighting chemistry, tension, and growth in your narrative!

Best Matches

"The Motivated Hard-Working Man is Best Suited for...The Strategic Creative Woman"

Who is She?

She is always thinking several steps ahead. Her ambitions aren't limited to small wins—she dreams big. Whether it's in launching a business, championing social causes, or setting bold personal development milestones, her mind is constantly imagining transformative outcomes, not just incremental change. She doesn't simply climb the ladder—she rebuilds the ladder and reconfigures what it should look like!

This forward-thinking drive fuels her even in the face of resistance or failure. She thrives where others may retreat or hesitate while maintaining momentum through clarity of purpose and an unshakable belief in what's possible. Her visionary mindset often inspires those around her to dream bigger and operate beyond conventional limits.

At the core of her strength is exceptional organization and her resourcefulness in most circumstances. She is a master planner—whether orchestrating events, managing complex projects, or navigating unexpected setbacks. She has a sharp eye for detail, knows how to delegate wisely, and never compromises on quality. Challenges don't paralyze her—they activate her. She quickly pivots, taps into her well of knowledge, or learns what she doesn't yet know to get the job done. Her balance of creativity and structure allows her to turn ambitious dreams into real, tangible success.

But what truly sets her apart is her high emotional intelligence. Her ambition is never cold or disconnected. She's deeply aware of how her actions affect others and places high value on relationships. She reads people well, listens with empathy, and builds genuine trust. She's often the emotional compass in teams—identifying tension early, addressing conflict tactfully, and ensuring everyone feels valued. Her compassion makes her leadership not just effective—but magnetic for all those she encounters!

In short, she is a force of nature: a woman who leads with vision, operates precisely, and connects with passion and heart.

Why They Work

When two ambitious, goal-driven individuals come together in a relationship, they form a rare and powerful bond rooted in love and mutual vision. These partners fuel each other's drive, celebrate each other's wins, and offer thoughtful support when things get tough. They don't just want to succeed individually—they want to succeed together!

This kind of couple thrives on momentum and movement. Whether building careers, launching businesses, or setting personal development goals, they share a common language of structure, strategy, and following through, irrespective of any challenges. They map out objectives, divide responsibilities, and track their progress like a high-performing team. Their connection becomes a source of strength—not just an emotional one, but a practical one. Friends and peers often see them as a couple that truly *gets things done*!

Due to their strengths seamlessly complementing each other, their relationship becomes a launchpad for growth and fruitfulness. She brings vision and precision to the relationship, while he similarly contributes discipline and drive. Together, they create a synergy that turns big dreams into tangible accomplishments.

Yet, with this power comes a challenge: the risk of ambition burnout. When both people are constantly working and in motion, it's easy for romance and rest to take a backseat in their relationship. Long hours, packed schedules, and never-ending checklists can leave little room for emotional intimacy or simple joy.

That's why they must intentionally protect their connection—through unplugged date nights, weekend getaways, or even just 30-minute coffee talks where work is off-limits. These pauses are not distractions but essential fuel for the long haul. When this couple remembers to nourish their relationship with the same energy they pour into their goals, their bond becomes unstoppable.

"The Passionate Dreamer Man is Best Suited for... Stable and Empathic Woman"

Who is She?

She is the kind of woman whose gentle presence brings comfort and calm to any situation. Deeply compassionate and emotionally attuned, she shows up fully when others struggle—not to fix everything, but to listen, validate her loved ones, and simply to *be there*. Her empathy runs deep, making her a safe place for honest conversations, quiet tears, or moments of doubt.

But make no mistake—her softness is not to be misconstrued for weakness. She balances her emotional warmth with grounded wisdom. Whether managing a home, navigating schedules, or handling life's practical tasks, she does so with quiet strength. She knows genuine compassion isn't just about feelings and making sound decisions supporting long-term well-being. Structure, for her, is a form of love.

Her gift lies in encouraging growth without pushing too hard. She's not interested in fast success or flashy results. Instead, she gently nurtures ambition—reminding her partner of their goals while helping them stay grounded in what's genuinely doable. She doesn't just believe in big dreams; she believes in the steps necessary to make those dreams a reality!

In a relationship, her patience and support create a peaceful rhythm. She helps maintain emotional balance, keeps life running smoothly, and reminds her partner of what really matters. Love is steady, thoughtful, and deeply nourishing with her—a partnership supporting the heart and the home.

Why They Work

Their bond is rooted in deep emotional connections, where vulnerability is not feared but surprisingly welcomed. Whether unpacking life's worries or celebrating the beauty in a quiet moment, they both value the intimacy that comes from truly being seen and heard. Their relationship feels safe, sincere, and emotionally rich—where love is spoken authentically in quiet gestures and heartfelt words.

One of the most inspiring aspects of their connection is the creative flow they share. He brings light, poetry, and big, romantic ideas to the table. She brings gentle structure and calm support, helping his dreams take shape without overwhelming his spirit. He thrives under her quiet encouragement, and she delights in the world he invites her into—full of art, imagination, and meaning.

Together, they form a beautiful blend of inspiration and stability—where neither practicality nor passion is sacrificed.

She ensures the bills get paid and the fridge is stocked. He ensures that the love notes and messages in a bottle keep coming and that life never loses its zest. It's a relationship that nourishes the soul while simultaneously tending to real-world needs.

Still, the balance isn't always easy. He might feel like his dreams aren't taken seriously if she leans too hard into a routine. Suppose he becomes lost in fantasy or overly ambitious plans. She might feel burdened by trying to hold it all together in that case. The key is communication—acknowledging one another's strengths and staying grounded in mutual appreciation.

When they honor both heart and home, their love becomes a rare and radiant partnership, anchored in dreams and reality … yet lifted and fueled by love.

3

"The Dependable – Peacekeeper Man is Best Suited for…The Nurturing and Creative Woman"

Who is She?

This is a woman who genuinely radiates kindness in everything that she does. Whether preparing a meal for a loved one, volunteering at a local shelter, or simply being a shoulder to lean on her natural instinct is to care deeply. Compassion isn't just something she offers in moments of crisis—it's a way of life. She wants to make the world more welcoming and more humane—one thoughtful act at a time.

But don't mistake her gentle heart for a lack of direction. She is deeply purpose-driven. Behind her nurturing spirit lies a fire to build something meaningful—a cause, community, and creative expression reflecting her values. She may dream of launching a nonprofit, opening a healing space, writing a book, or leading a grassroots movement. Her compassion isn't passive—but proactively fuels her mission.

She blends her idealism with steady resolve. When she sets her mind on something, she follows through. Her commitment is quiet but formidably unwavering, grounded in a desire to serve and grow. She's not looking for a spotlight or status—just real impact.

In relationships, she offers deep emotional support and loyalty. But she also needs space to grow, lead, and pursue the goals that give her life meaning. She thrives best with someone who respects both her tenderness and her tenacity.

Her adaptability helps her pivot when needed, yet she never loses sight of her core values. She knows how to hold space for change while remaining anchored in truth. This makes her resilient and wise—able to face life's turns with heart and grit.

Why They Work

Together, the two create a beautifully grounded partnership where warmth meets stability and dreams are built on a strong foundation. He offers the quiet strength of consistency and loyalty while providing an emotional anchor that gives her space to feel safe, secure, and seen. She, in turn, brings depth and heart, infusing their home with emotional richness, shared purpose, and a nurturing spirit.

Their love becomes a safe haven—a place to rest, reflect, and recharge from the world's demands. Whether it's a cozy Sunday dinner or a shared goal on the horizon, their everyday connection is full of comfort and intentionality.

But this isn't just a domestic love—it's a mission-aligned bond. She dreams boldly. He grounds those dreams. She sees what could be. He knows how to build step-by-step. When she feels overwhelmed by the big picture, he can help to break it down. When he starts playing it too safe, she gently encourages him to take a chance or leap of faith. Together, they balance their aspirations with realism, creating forward momentum without sacrificing peace.

Still, their greatest strength—routine and emotional security—can also become a trap. If predictability becomes too dominant, it may stifle her creative spark or make growth feel stagnated. On the other hand, when her visionary drive urges quick, bold changes, he may hesitate, needing what he thinks is the appropriate amount of time to weigh the risks.

The solution lies in continuous mutual understanding. They avoid stagnation and thrive as a team by honoring each other's pace and perspective. His steadiness doesn't have to mean standing still. Her ambition doesn't need to be rushed. Instead, their love becomes what it was always meant to be: a launching pad for purpose, a sanctuary for healing, and a strengthened partnership with every season.

"The Thrill-Seeker Man is Best Suited for...The Curious Explorer Woman"

Who is She?

She is the perfect blend of open-hearted curiosity and thoughtful awareness. Enthusiastic about new experiences, she's drawn to life's endless possibilities—whether it's exploring a hidden beach town, diving into a new book on philosophy, or trying out an exotic dish. Yet, unlike someone driven solely by impulse, she brings a measured confidence to her adventurous spirit, allowing her to say "yes" to life while staying rooted in common sense.

Her balance between independence and connection with others makes her stand out. She values her space and solitude to escape love and reconnect with herself. Whether journaling, working toward a personal goal, or savoring a quiet morning with coffee, she finds joy in solitude. However, when she returns to her partner, circle, or village, she does so with a renewed presence and appreciative spirit.

In relationships, she thrives best when mutual respect for freedom, autonomy, and emotional closeness exists. She doesn't need constant oversight to feel loved; instead, she seeks a partnership where both can chase dreams, explore the world, and still come home to each other's arms.

Her practical nature means that even her most spontaneous ideas come with a plan. She's the one who books the flight, double-checks the reservations, and still surprises you with a scenic detour. She lives for the thrill of adventure—but with both feet planted firmly on the ground.

This makes her an ideal match for a Thrill-Seeker who needs someone to embrace the excitement and create a soft place to land. With her, exploration becomes more than escapism—it becomes meaningful, intentional, and shared.

Why They Work

Their connection is fueled by curiosity, spontaneity, and a shared zest for life. From impromptu road trips to sporadic museum visits or learning a new skill together, they thrive on experiences pushing mundane routines' boundaries. Their mutual love of discovery keeps their relationship exciting, vibrant, and ever-evolving—thus, a beautiful dance between freedom and connection.

She brings thoughtful intention to their journey, anchoring their adventures with practicality and foresight. While he dreams up their next escapade, she's making sure they've packed snacks, checked the forecast, and set the GPS. This harmony between her grounded energy and his free spirit keeps their life together exciting but not overwhelming.

Together, they dream big and move boldly, yet they do so with balance and ease. She tempers risk with intuition. He encourages her to stretch beyond the familiar and predictable. Their dynamic is magnetic—alive with movement, learning, laughter, and shared stories.

Still, they must be mindful of pausing long enough to plant and grow their roots. While the thrill of the new can be exhilarating, emotional depth often builds during quieter, long-lasting, and more intentional moments. Slowing down to reflect collectively, setting shared goals, or simply sitting still together is essential in ensuring that their relationship matures while experiencing these adventures.

With a little structure and ongoing emotional check-ins, this duo can enjoy a love story rich in exploration and steady enough to last a lifetime.

"The Intellect Philosopher Man is Best Suited for...The Thoughtful and Innovative Woman"

Who is She?

She is a woman whose mind lives in layers of meaningfulness, imagination, and emotional truth. Whether she's sketching ideas in the margins of a journal, meandering through a quiet art exhibit, or lost in thought, she sees life through a lens of possibility and beauty. Her creativity doesn't just live in projects—it colors how she views relationships, decisions, and even the quietest moments of the day.

What sets her apart is the way she blends insight with empathy. She can read between the lines—not just in books, but intuitively in people. She senses when someone is off before they say a word. She understands the weight of unspoken words and the meaning behind subtle gestures. Her presence is comforting and thought-provoking, inviting those around her to feel and think more deeply.

She doesn't crave the spotlight. Instead, she prefers meaningful conversations over small talk, depth over flashiness, and authenticity over approval. Her calm demeanor gives her a quiet power—when she speaks, it's because she has something real and substantive to say. Similarly, when she listens, she listens with her whole heart.

However, please don't make the mistake of confusing her quietness for passivity or meekness. Her inner world is alive with passion, ideas, and endless curiosity. When inspiration strikes, it moves through her like electricity—infusing her work, relationships, and self-expression with soulful energy.

She is the perfect complement to a partner who values intellectual and emotional depth, someone who delights in dialogue, reflection, and shared wonder. Life becomes a rich tapestry of thought, emotion, and meaning with her. This slow-burning flame warms, illuminates, and inspires others.

Why They Work

Their connection is rooted in the meeting of minds—a partnership built on insight, introspection, and a shared reverence for knowledge and life's meaning. From intimate late-night talks on human nature to quiet moments spent reading side-by-side, they thrive in a space where thoughts and feelings are honored equally.

Together, they create an intellectual sanctuary—a space where curiosity is never dismissed and wonder is always welcome. Their conversations range from art, faith, and science to philosophy and psychology while reflecting their shared desire to understand life, not just live it. He brings clarity and structure. She brings nuance and soul. He dissects ideas with precision; she expands them with imagination.

It's in this give-and-take song and dance that their relationship continues to flourish and abide. She gently nudges him toward emotional expressions and creative exploration, helping him soften his sharp logic with empathy. In return, he gives her stability—an invaluable framework through which her ideas and insights can blossom.

Yet, even the most brilliant minds can drift too far into abstraction. Their challenge is remembering that love is not just a concept to be understood—but an experience to be felt, cultivated, nurtured, and lived! When life becomes too heavy, they must ground themselves in the present—through touch, acts of care, shared routines, and even the smallest of joys!

When they conquer this, their connection becomes more than an intellectual one—deeply intimate, intellectually satisfying, and emotionally fulfilling—a true partnership of heart, body, mind, and soul.

"A Short Quiz to Check Your Possible Match"

Note: This short quiz is not designed to match you with your ideal partner perfectly. Instead, it serves as a gentle starting point—an invitation to begin thinking in the right direction regarding love, compatibility, and emotional connection.

In the **next chapter**, you'll find additional resources, reflections, and a deeper analysis to help you understand your patterns and preferences more clearly. This deeper insight will guide you toward making more intentional and fulfilling relationship choices.

1. What do you value most in a partner?

A. Ambition and stability

B. Romance and emotional depth

C. Loyalty and peace

D. Adventure and spontaneity

E. Deep conversation and wisdom

2. How do you prefer to spend quality time together?

A. Planning and building a future

B. Sharing dreams and heartfelt talks

C. Relaxing at home with emotional safety

D. Exploring new places or trying new things

E. Debating ideas or watching thought-provoking documentaries

3. What do you admire most in a man?

A. His drive and discipline

B. His emotional expressiveness

C. His reliability and patience

D. His boldness and zest for life

E. His intelligence and insight

If Your Answers Are ......

- Mostly A's → Your ideal match is the **Motivated Hard worker.**

- Mostly B's → Your ideal match is the **Passionate Dreamer.**

- Mostly C's → Your ideal match is the **Dependable Peacekeeper.**

- Mostly D's → Your ideal match is the **Thrill-Seeker**

- Mostly E's → Your ideal match is the **Intellect Philosopher.**

Additional Resources

As you continue your journey toward self-awareness, emotional healing, and meaningful relationships, it's important to know that the work doesn't stop here. The insights in this book are only the beginning.

Whether you're working through unresolved past emotional wounds, seeking to understand the male perspective more deeply, or learning how to create a relationship that aligns with your values, many tools are available to support your growth.

For women seeking to understand emotional intelligence and healing from trauma better, *The Body Keeps the Score* by Dr. Bessel van der Kolk and *How to Do the Work* by Dr. Nicole LePera are powerful guides that explore the connection between past experiences and present behaviors.

These books are invaluable for breaking generational cycles, processing emotional pain, and beginning the journey toward wholeness. If you want to improve your self-awareness and understand how emotions function, *Emotional Intelligence* by Daniel Goleman and *Atlas of the Heart* by Brené Brown are transformative reads that unpack the science and stories behind how we feel, communicate, and connect.

When it comes to love and relationships, understanding your attachment style can change everything. *Attached* by Amir

Levine and Rachel Heller, it offers a science-backed look into why we bond the way we do and how to form healthier connections.

Dr. Sue Johnson's Hold Me Tight and Love Sense provide practical tools to create more meaningful emotional bonds for those craving deeper emotional intimacy in their relationships.

In understanding men, masculinity, and archetypes, *King, Warrior, Magician, Lover* by Robert Moore and Douglas Gillette, and The Way of the Superior Man by David Deida offer powerful insights into the inner lives of men—their desires, emotional needs, and the silent burdens they carry.

For women ultimately wanting to explore their feminine power, identity, and influence, *The Queen's Code* by Alison Armstrong and *Women Who Run with the Wolves* by Clarissa Pinkola Estés offer encouragement and wisdom drawn from modern insight and ancient stories.

Modern dating has changed dramatically, and resources like *Modern Romance* by Aziz Ansari and *The Defining Decade* by Meg Jay provide relevant perspectives for women navigating love in a tech-driven, fast-paced world.

If you want to learn about healthy dating boundaries, communication, and understanding the male mind, consider listening to podcasts like "Dear Future Wifey" by Laterras R. Whitfield and content from dating coaches like Stephan Speaks or Matthew Hussey.

Suppose you're more of a hands-on learner. In that case, excellent tools like the Attachment Style Quiz from The Attachment Project, shadow work journals, and self-discovery planners allow you to dig deeper. These are ideal for personal reflection, emotional tracking, and staying committed to personal development outside therapy or coaching sessions.

Above all, the most important resource is your willingness to grow. Ask questions, seek truth, and listen to your heart and history. The more you understand where you've been and how you've been shaped, the better equipped you are to choose a future aligned with your values—and the kind of love that not only complements you but truly and completely... nourishes you.